Praise for *What a Girl Wants*

'This is the book I wish existed when I was younger, all told in Roxy's wonderful, unique, inimitable way. Roxy has my heart.' – Adele Roberts, broadcaster and author

'I LOVED *What a Girl Wants* – courageous, moving, bold and beautifully, brilliantly written. I think readers are going to be reaching for this for years to come – it's a memoir that encourages us all to step into ourselves and celebrate who we are.' – Daisy Buchanan, author of *Limelight, Careering* and *Pity Party*

'Smart and funny – genuinely brilliantly, laugh out loud funny. *What a Girl Wants* is unabashed, bold, even confronting at times and it's exhilarating to read Roxy's words, to be witness to her life.' – Laura Kay, author of *The Split, Making It* and *Tell Me Everything*

'An inspiring and refreshing read! I wish this had been around when I was 19. And 29, and 39 . . .' – Val McDermid, author of the Karen Pirie and Wire in the Blood series

'Brilliant and relatable. Wonderfully honest, a joy to read. Every queer woman NEEDS to own this. I'm immediately buying a copy for every single queer woman I know . . . that's a lot of copies.' – Rosie Jones, comedian and author

'A riot of a book from a leading LGBT literary talent: hilarious, soulful and true.' – Joelle Taylor, poet, playwright and author of *The Night Alphabet* and *C+nto & Othered Poems*

'I adored *What a Girl Wants*. It's such a lovely, warm book to escape to. It gave me so much joy.' – Kate Holderness, actor and author

'Brilliant! Beautiful, kind, inclusive, hilarious, passionate. Read this book. It's a taster of how glorious things can be when a girl gets what she wants.' – Rachel Shelley, actor, broadcaster and star of *The L Word*

'A delicious account of learning to love who you really are. Heartfelt, sexy and highly entertaining, Roxy Bourdillon's memoir is also tender on the realities of growing up queer and what it means to be out and proud today.' – Holly Williams, author of *The Start of Something* and *What Time is Love?*

'How can you read with tears in your eyes? Roxy Bourdillon is a born survivor whose brave memoir is an honest, uplifting and inspirational journey of discovery. I loved it!' – Mari Hannah, author of the Kate Daniels and Stone & Oliver series

'*What a Girl Wants* is a warm, tender, and playful memoir of growing up lesbian all the way up to becoming the *DIVA* magazine editor-in-chief. Roxy Bourdillon has a wonderfully natural and friendly voice, it was so easy to want to pick it back up and keep reading.' – Lily Lindon, author of *Double Booked* and *My Own Worst Enemy*

What a Girl Wants

A (True) Story of Sexuality
and Self-discovery

ROXY BOURDILLON

What a Girl Wants

A (True) Story of Sexuality and Self-discovery

BLUEBIRD

First published 2025 by Bluebird
an imprint of Pan Macmillan
The Smithson, 6 Briset Street, London EC1M 5NR
EU representative: Macmillan Publishers Ireland Ltd, 1st Floor,
The Liffey Trust Centre, 117–126 Sheriff Street Upper,
Dublin 1, DO1 YC43
Associated companies throughout the world
www.panmacmillan.com

ISBN 978-1-0350-3715-5

1 3 5 7 9 8 6 4 2

A CIP catalogue record for this book is available from the British Library.

Typeset in Freight Text Pro by
Palimpsest Book Production Ltd, Falkirk, Stirlingshire

Printed and bound by CPI Group (UK) Ltd, Croydon, CRO 4YY

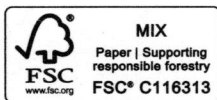

MIX
Paper | Supporting
responsible forestry
FSC
www.fsc.org FSC® C116313

Visit **www.panmacmillan.com/bluebird** to read more about all our books
and to buy them. You will also find features, author interviews and
news of any author events, and you can sign up for e-newsletters
so that you're always first to hear about our new releases.

For Granny Nancy, with love

Author's note

Some of the names and minor details in this book have been changed to protect those who never imagined they might someday end up in my memoir. This book is based on my own memories of a specific period in my life. Of course, other people may remember things differently and have their own reasons for their actions. I can only tell you mine. So what lies ahead is a very personal story about what it was really like for me, growing up and moving through this world as a woman, who really, *really* loves women.

Contents

Welcome   1

CHAPTER 1:   Origins of a people-pleaser   7

CHAPTER 2:   I kissed a girl   19

CHAPTER 3:   A bit about boys and girls   29

CHAPTER 4:   Experimenting with heterosexuality   43

CHAPTER 5:   Talking, laughing, loving, breathing, fighting, fucking   53

CHAPTER 6:   Undercover queer   65

CHAPTER 7:   The truth about coming out   79

CHAPTER 8:   Get the party started   95

CHAPTER 9:   Rainbow glitter! Drag queens! DYKES ON BIKES!!   101

CHAPTER 10:   The Clothes   115

CHAPTER 11:   What happens when my heart breaks   129

CHAPTER 12:   Suddenly single   139

CHAPTER 13:   I love women's bodies, but can I love my own?   151

CHAPTER 14:   Hello, Brenda! The gay lady dating scene and other magical, soul-destroying things   161

CHAPTER 15:   Yes, it counts!   **171**

CHAPTER 16:   This should not be normal   **183**

CHAPTER 17:   Goodbyes and hellos   **197**

CHAPTER 18:   How to fall in love when your   **207**
              heart is broken

CHAPTER 19:   Something must change   **221**

CHAPTER 20:   The dawn of a new DIVA   **231**

CHAPTER 21:   The power of community   **241**

CHAPTER 22:   What this girl wants   **251**

              Epilogue   **255**

              Acknowledgements   **259**

Welcome

I am thirteen years old and these are my secrets:

1. I have a crush on Jet from ITV gameshow *Gladiators*. *So strong! So pretty!*
2. I still play with Barbie dolls. It's mostly making them scissor. Or snog. Or lie on top of each other with feeling.
3. I just kissed my best friend. Spoiler alert: she's a girl.

If you're a fellow queer, I'm so happy you're here. If you're straight, I am equally delighted to meet you. You seem lovely! You absolutely don't have to be gay to enjoy this book. In fact, many of the experiences I've had in life have been far more shaped by my gender than my sexuality. This book is for you if you are interested in people, have a sense of humour and love women, and that doesn't have to be in a romantic or sexual way. Woman-lovers of all kinds are welcome in these pages.

For me, though, the sapphic signs are there right from the start. I have Feelings with a capital F for girls and I simply don't have those same Feelings for boys. Yet I don't come out, even to myself, for a decade. What can I say? Compulsory heterosexuality is a powerful overlord. Plus, it's the late nineties and we are tits-deep in Section 28, the poisonous Tory law banning teachers from the 'promotion of homosexuality', i.e. saying anything that might suggest even for a millisecond that being queer isn't The Absolute Worst Thing That Can Happen to You.

Speaking of tits, I wake up one morning in my thirteenth year and make an alarming discovery. Two juggernauts have erupted on my previously flat chest. This is disconcerting.

Woah, where did the babylons come from? What am I meant to DO with them? Do I need a licence for these wobbling weapons of mass destruction?

It is not an exaggeration to say that becoming an overnight member of the Massive Titty Committee changes the way I am treated by other people for the rest of my life. There's a time BC, Before Cleavage, and AD, After D-cups.

Society assumes that we are all straight, right? Well, society takes one look at my great big jubblies and also assumes that I am 'up for it', 'a bit of a goer' and not just straight, but 'absolutely gagging for a fella'. THIS IS ALL VERY CONFUSING! I JUST WANT TO GO AND WATCH *GLADIATORS* AGAIN!

Most of my classmates are boy crazy, but I'm so reluctant to kiss one I'm branded 'frigid' by my peers. Also 'slutty', on account of the whoppers. What's that I can smell? Ah, yes. It's patriarchal bullshit!

Instead of devoting any serious thought to what my enthusiastic lady-snogging might mean, I decide that my ardent passion for all womankind is simply because I'm a feminist. I become the world's most devoted fan of an entire gender. I voluntarily do a school project on women's rights. I make scrapbooks filled with pages ripped from magazines picturing feisty-looking ladies. I painstakingly curate mixtapes exclusively featuring bands with the word 'girls' in their name (Spice

Girls, Girls Aloud, Cheeky Girls). And the truth is I am a feminist. I'm also a raging lesbian. But I am running purely on instinct right now. To kiss another girl is instinctive. To keep it quiet is too.

Because nobody considers that I might be anything other than straight, they are often horrifically homophobic right in front of me. This does not make me eager to burst out of the closet and declare my truest self anytime soon.

The first time I see a lesbian on TV, she is in prison. The show is ITV drama *Bad Girls*, all about bad girls doing bad, and occasionally gay, things behind bars. According to the world presented to me on-screen, straight people get to be CEOs and superheroes and princesses. Lesbians are criminals.

I read Radclyffe Hall's infamous 1928 novel, *The Well of Loneliness*, a book, ironically, I pick up to feel less alone. Prior to this, I'd been under the impression the twenties were all about doing the Charleston, getting a bob and larking around saying, 'Tally ho, old chap.' I had my fingers crossed for an upbeat romcom starring flappers flapping about with each other's flaps, wearing nothing but a feather headband and a brazen smile. Instead, our leading lesbian is drowning in the misery of unrequited love and being told obscenely homophobic things like, 'I'd like to institute state lethal chambers.' Being a 'degenerate' isn't half as much fun as it sounds. I probably should have twigged from the title.

Then something marvellous happens. I stumble upon the sumptuous BBC adaptation of Sarah Waters' sapphic historical romance, *Tipping the Velvet*. Things start to perk up, literally. I am staggered, spellbound and slightly aroused as I watch main character Nan King, starkers save for a layer of gold body paint and a terrifyingly girthy strap-on, at what appears to be a decadent Victorian orgy for eccentric lesbian millionaires. It's hard to tear my eyes away from the nineteenth-century sex toy, affectionately referred to as 'Monsieur Dildo'. *Ring-a-ding-ding, this is more like it!*

Spurred on by this delicious nugget of saucy, queer joy, I track down a copy of the lesbian magazine *DIVA*, in WHSmith at Leeds train station. No eye contact is made during the purchase transaction. Surreptitiously, I slip my contraband inside *Cosmopolitan* as a disguise to the outside world, lest anyone might notice my actual reading material and deduce that I'm a colossal dyke. So essentially, *Cosmo* is *DIVA*'s beard. I practically inhale the issue and become a dedicated covert reader, poring over every copy I can get my mitts on, especially the Sex Issues. The women in here aren't convicts or vintage-gold-dildo-connoisseurs (alas). No, they are everyday people, who are really into cats, k.d. lang and performing cunnilingus on their girlfriends. I love this for them. Yet still, I stay closeted. Yet still, the queer treasures I am collecting are shrouded in a very private shame.

But this book isn't just about me getting to grips with being gay. There's a lot more to me than my sexuality, and there's a lot more to *What a Girl Wants* than that, too. What follows is an honest account of what it's really like for me growing up, battling misogyny, attempting to find peace within my unruly body and struggling to achieve my burning yet seemingly impossible dream of a creative career. It includes my most audacious adventures, my cringe-making moments and the crushing devastation of heartbreak. It's a love letter to the defining women in my life, and most of them are not romantic partners. They are my closest friends who pick me up when I am down, and my spectacular grandmother, who shapes who I am in so many ways, from inspiring my adoration for vintage style to informing my understanding of how to live a good, fulfilling life.

Fast forward to the present day and I am now out of the

closet in a major way. Not only because I live with my lovely longtime girlfriend, but through my job as editor-in-chief of *DIVA* – yes, the same magazine I used to read on the sly. This book documents my journey from closeted lezza to professional queer. My younger self would be shocked to learn that I am now paid to write about, to use the technical industry term, 'gay stuff'. I have very much monetized my homosexuality. Gay for pay all the way, that's me. I don't just lesbian, I lesbian for a living. (To clarify, I also lesbian in my free time.)

Since my days as a horny, angst-ridden teenager, I have witnessed a queer revolution. Unlike when I was thirteen, thanks to the work of tireless activists, gay people can now get hitched and more of us than ever are proudly claiming our LGBTQIA identities. Lena Waithe is on the red carpet resplendent in a Pride flag cape. Hayley Kiyoko is being crowned Lesbian Jesus and saving us all through homoerotic music videos. Even Velma from *Scooby Doo* is at it. She's finally come out of the closet, causing #lesbian to trend on social media.

I am so here for all of this. We need these moments of triumphant fabulousness and we should certainly celebrate how far we've come. But my god, it is alarmingly apparent that there is still so much further to go for queer people and all women, from eradicating inequality and abuse to repairing fault lines within our own ranks. While doing this vital, gruelling work, we are also faced with the daunting task of trying to understand and embrace ourselves. So how do we make the necessary strides forward? That is one of the questions I will attempt to answer in this book.

But at its core, this book is about sharing my own personal story. It's about charting my experience as a woman, who happens to really, *really* love women, in a world that can sometimes make you feel terrible about both of those things. It's about the messy, complicated, joyful business of figuring out who I am and untangling what I'm told I should want from what I actually desire. From body image and mental health to love and loss, it's all in here and it's all straight from my heart.

However you identify, you deserve to feel seen, empowered and entertained. To this end, I'm very happy to offer up tales of my own personal humili*gay*tions and wow, there have been a *lot* of those. When we laugh, we feel less lonely. When you read the following pages it is my hope that you know that, despite how it may sometimes seem, you are not alone. You are part of a wonderful, inspiring, outrageously good-looking family of women, queer folks and our amazing friends. And you should never, ever, under *any* circumstances, be made to feel bad about having outstanding taste in celebrity crushes.

CHAPTER 1

Origins of a people-pleaser

I'm in my granny's kitchen. We're performing our usual post-dinner ritual. She is doing the dishes, I am on drying duty. Over the suds of Fairy Liquid as the sunlight dwindles to dusk through the window, we are, as we always do when it's just the two of us, putting the world to rights.

I am ten years old, with chubby, rosy cheeks and teeth that splay out in opposite directions. There is eczema ravaging the backs of my knees and the creases of my elbows, prompting other kids to stage-whisper that I have fleas. I am a prime target for bullies. One boy from school has taken to standing by my gate and singing, for all my neighbours to hear, about how fat I am. This humiliates me beyond measure. I'm not what you would describe as one of life's winners. I am bright, though, and bookish, top of the class in every subject except P.E. I love reading and writing. Spending great swathes of time alone, I craft intricate paper magazines, create my own hand-illustrated story books, and record rambling, pretend radio shows on the cassette player.

Part shy girl, part show-off, this dichotomy rages within me and I lurch awkwardly between the two extremes. At times I'm so overwhelmed with anxiety at the mere thought of being around other people, at the horrifying prospect of them bearing witness to my monstrous appearance, I claw at my rashy skin until it bleeds red rivers down my limbs. At other times, seized with sudden verve, I might burst into an impromptu, wildly inappropriate musical turn in front of bemused onlookers. For some unknown reason, during one trip to the park I decide to leap up onto a bench and break out a solo rendition of Madonna's 'Hanky Panky'. I don't know all the words, but I know the most important line like the back of my tiny, messed-up child hand, so I sing about a good spank(y) on repeat. I accompany this refrain with a primitive version of the 'Macarena'.

I simultaneously fear and crave attention. My granny seems to understand this central contradiction in me. Many of our conversations, when we're not talking about our favourite fashions and the books we're currently reading, are discussions about the nuances of human nature.

She passes me a serving dish to dry with my damp tea towel. She reminds me, as she often does, about her memory of an incident that illustrates my two competing inner forces succinctly. Apparently, when I was a very little girl I was asked to recite a poem at a family gathering. I took this request preposterously seriously, my little face immediately awash with anxiety. Nevertheless, I marched myself off alone into the corner of the room. She watched on with interest as I visibly wrestled with the enormity of the task, obviously feeling extreme pressure, putting so much pressure on myself even as a kid. But then, all of a sudden, I seemed to grasp hold of myself. Taking a deep, momentous breath, I performed my poem with astounding fervour. I conjured the sudden illusion of unshakeable confidence and pizazz, despite having clearly just been through a private, torturous ordeal. That is me in a nutshell. An ugly duckling who occasionally musters the guts to momentarily make-believe I'm a majestic swan. I'm a right little oddbod, yet here I am smiling, glowing, because I am with my granny and she is the absolute queen of my world.

Unlike ungainly, geeky little me, she is elegance and charm personified. She's so glamorous, it's like having a movie star in the family. She is the Grace Kelly of grandmothers. She's kind too, thoughtful, funny and idiosyncratic. She pronounces 'hummus' 'hoo-moss' and 'tuna fish' 'tunnuh fish'. How she makes me giggle. Her catchphrases include 'I shouldn't tell you this . . . but' said conspiratorially before delivering a juicy morsel of gossip, and 'Now I put it in a safe place', only ever said when she's lost something. She plays the piano, loves to dance and lights up every room she enters. For me at ten years old, to be near my granny is to be in the presence of the divine. I love the rest of my family greatly, but this is the relationship that sparkles the brightest and soothes me the most. It is the least complicated, unmarred by resentments or disappointments or hurt feelings. It is so full of warmth and light and verve, of shared passions and mutual silliness, of deep discussion and even deeper love.

As I organize the clean cutlery into the correct dividers in its wooden drawer, our conversation turns, as it frequently does when we're alone, to the state of my parents' marriage. Naturally my granny worries about her daughter, my mum. She wants her to be happy with her husband, as she is with my grandad, and yet my mum is so clearly unhappy. Both my parents are. We lament the sadness of their situation. We dissect the many ways in which they are blatantly incompatible, how she is an extrovert and he is a textbook introvert. We talk about what a shame it is that they seem to bring out the worst in each other.

Feeling philosophical, I turn to my granny and say sagely, like a primary school Yoda, that I think that most people are doing their best with their own limited experience of the world. She looks at me, marvelling at my observation, even though we've had a variation of this same conversation at least half a dozen times before. 'Aren't you wise,' she says earnestly. She often tells me this and every time she does, I puff up like I've won a prize.

This is my safe, happy place. My grandparents' house is in York, only half an hour from my family home, so I visit often and stay over at weekends. Unlike the place where I live, this house is warm, clean and cosy. It's full of laughter, love and routine. My grandparents' home is my sanctuary. Here, domestic life takes on a reassuring rhythm. There is a comforting shape to it all.

Every morning begins with the sounds of Grandad clattering in the kitchen, preparing breakfast with Classic FM on the radio. He serves Granny breakfast in bed and I snuggle up beside her under her floral quilt, chatting away as she dines from her tray, like the queen she is. Our days are filled with wholesome trips to the library or the park. Homecooked meals are eaten together at the dining room table, with separate serving bowls for meat, potatoes and veg. After dinner I'm allowed to choose a chocolate from Granny's box of Milk Tray, a permanent fixture on the shelf next to her armchair, restocked by Grandad as required. I always agonize over this decision. I always choose the Strawberry Cream. Afterwards perhaps we'll have a game of Scrabble or gin rummy. Then hot cocoa and a bubble bath before bed. It all sounds so simple, but to me the domestic structure of these visits is bliss. It could not be more different from the house where I actually live.

My family home is cold, run-down and, at times, frightening. I rarely invite friends round because I am embarrassed of the literal and emotional mess that is scattered everywhere. This house is the battleground of a vicious adult war that has been raging for years. My parents' marriage is desperately, catastrophically unhappy. It has been this way for as long as I can remember. At ten years old, it feels like it has been this way forever. Their misery has never been hidden from me. Not once have I, at any age, been under the illusion that we are, or have ever been, a happy family.

Growing up, I am never encouraged to believe in my parents' marriage, just as I am never told that Santa is real. When I start school, I hear classmates talking excitedly about this Father Christmas fella. I go home and tentatively broach the subject, transparently angling for more gifts under the tree. My mum shuts down any suggestion of a benevolent man in a jolly red coat hurtling down our chimney. The message is: 'I'm not having an imaginary beardy bloke taking credit for presents I bought and paid for.' Which is fair enough and difficult to argue with. Just as I learn that the sky is blue and the grass is green and Santa is a sham, so I learn that my mum and dad detest each other. It is one of the unavoidable facts of life.

Another fact of life? They will one day divorce. Exactly when this will happen is to be determined by my age. Talk about feeling pressure to grow up fast! I am a ticking time bomb, their unsigned decree absolute in human form, the reason they feel obligated to stay stuck in such a miserable situation. At first, I am told that when I am eighteen, they will split. Then it is to happen when I reach sixteen. Finally, it is decided that their marriage will be done as soon as I turn eleven.

As a child I hear phrases bandied about on TV. People talk about 'staying together for the children' and I think at the time how misguided this sentiment is, at least in my case. I don't want my parents to be unhappy. I certainly don't want to be the reason they feel duty-bound to remain in such torment.

After years of anguish, their pain, our collective family pain, is baked into the walls of every room of our house. I can feel the weight of it in the air. And so, I learn to tiptoe around it. Seeing my parents' unhappiness, I want to fix their pain. From a young age I feel it is my responsibility to manage the situation and minimize their suffering.

I learn tricks to defuse the tension and brighten the mood. My approach for each parent is tailored to them as an individual. With my dad, we never talk about The Great Unhappiness. He spends the majority of his days in the study with the door firmly shut. So I tentatively knock and, on his signal, enter for ten minutes at a time with one clear objective: to cheer up my downhearted dad. I play the fool to entertain him, sing daft, made-up songs, and call him 'Daddy Cool', which never fails to make him smile. I am my father's clown and my mother's counsellor. With her, The Great Unhappiness is very much up for discussion.

We talk about other things too, though. She is creative, playful and gives me the great gift of making learning fun. I discover that I can lift her spirits by getting high marks at school. Yet somehow, after a while, even this isn't enough to make her happy. One day I hurry home elated. I can't wait to tell my mum that I scored 97 per cent in an exam, the highest mark in the year. I declare my news in a flurry of boastful adrenaline. I am so sure that this will make her smile. Yet to my dismay, she does not look impressed or pleased. Instead she asks, in all seriousness, what happened to the other 3 per cent? And I am filled with shame over my suddenly measly mark. Shame that I have failed to achieve the absolute perfection she expects, the perfection I think she *needs*. Maybe she's just having a bad day. There are a lot of those. Whatever the reason, it doesn't change how I feel, because there is nothing I hate more than disappointing my parents, nothing I fear more than adding to their pain, nothing so crushing to me as the knowledge that I have failed to make them proud. And so I keep on trying, in whatever way I can, to bolster their spirits, soothe their sorrows and maintain the peace before everything inevitably blows up again.

In the future I will understand that I am a child caught in the crossfires of a grown-up situation. I will realize that the pressure of trying to hold back the dam of their adult pain is too much for one girl to bear, however wise beyond my years I may seem. I will see that it is all so much worse because I feel that I am the only one who can save them. Not save their marriage. This isn't *The Parent Trap*. This is real life, not a farcical film about kids playing matchmaker with their squabbling parents. I know that my parents' marriage is dead in the water. There is no point trying to save that, so instead I attempt to save them from their individual despair. I think, if I can just comfort them enough, please them enough, that if I am good enough, then perhaps it might make them happy.

By my eleventh birthday, they can't tolerate living under the same roof for a second longer. When they finally split up, I am relieved. My dad moves down South and I don't see him more than a handful of times a year after that. I stay with my mum, in our cold house with a decade of pain seeped into every surface, and attempt to console her.

I don't blame either of them for any of this, by the way. I don't as a child and I won't in the future when I'm grown up. I understand, have always understood, that they are two people, two people who I have vast oceans of love and compassion for, who are individually going through profound pain. It is obvious to me at ten years old and it will remain obvious to me for the rest of my days. I mean what I say to my granny. I know they are trying their best.

But it is also true that this is the arena in which my character starts to form. This is how I learn to shape-shift for the benefit of others. It is where my desperate need to please and keep the peace stems from. Of course, I am far from the only girl socialized to put other people's happiness before my own. Of course, this way of being will only be reinforced by the way our society treats women and girls. So many of us have been raised to be people-pleasers and pacifiers, if not by our family dynamics, then by the expectations and feminine ideals put on us: keep the peace, be a supplicant, be a good girl.

I sometimes wonder if my parents' clashing dispositions are the reason I have always had two such distinct sides to my own personality raging against each other within me. The show woman and the anxious recluse. Later on, I will question whether this juxtaposition is also tied up in me being gay, in longing to be seen but at the same time fearing, even fleeing it. But then I will think that maybe these contradictions are just what it is to be a complicated human being trying to navigate a confusing world.

My front-row ticket to the inner workings of a broken marriage is also where I form my initial understanding of what a romantic, or in my parents' case, decidedly unromantic, relationship looks like. Not a great first impression, I think we can agree. But the plot thickens. Because if Exhibit A is my parents' trainwreck of a union, Exhibit B is my granny and grandad, the most in-love couple you could ever hope to meet.

Like me, my grandad unequivocally adores my granny. I often catch him gazing at her before saying to the room, still entranced, 'Isn't she beautiful?' She cherishes him right back in return. Both dazzlingly charismatic, they are natural performers. The two of them have a husband-and-wife telepathy act. Yes, that's right. I literally have magic grandparents. Being soulmates is both the core tenet of their relationship and the USP of their onstage persona. Their tagline? 'Minds in harmony.' I love my grandad, am in awe of him really, but it's my granny who I'm closest to, who I feel that special, soul connection with. We are the ones who have so much in common. We are the ones who have hours of heart-to-hearts. Heart-to-hearts like the one we're having now at her kitchen sink.

We are discussing what makes a good marriage, a topic she is naturally the authority on. 'Friendship,' she declares. 'Grandad and I are great friends. We laugh together. We support each other.' I think to myself that if I ever do get married, I want a marriage like theirs. I doubt it will happen for me though. I'm not sure it's possible for love that spectacular to strike twice in the same family.

The dishes are all washed, dried and put away now. I look through the window and it is dark outside, but I am safe and warm and loved in this house with my gorgeous granny. Time for a few rounds of gin rummy, then hot cocoa and a bubble bath before bed.

A non-exhaustive list of on-screen moments that contribute to my lesbian awakening

The Cadbury Caramel Bunny advert in the 1980s and 90s
Surely one of the most seductive cartoon characters of all time, voiced by none other than lesbian icon Miriam Margolyes.

She-Ra in 1980s cartoon *He-Man and The Masters of The Universe*
By the power of Grayskull! He-Man's female counterpart, animated superhero and feminist icon. As a schoolgirl, I have a She-Ra quilt cover, so technically I get to cuddle up with her every night.

1990s kids' TV show *Mighty Morphin Power Rangers*
Specifically, the pink one.

Samantha Janus in 1990s ITV sitcom *Game On*
This one is not deep. Even as a child, I am mesmerized by Samantha's angel face.

Daria and her best friend Jane in 1990s animated teen series *Daria*
Sarcastic, rebellious, countercultural – are we sure these cartoon characters weren't actually a lesbian couple?

1999 high-school film *Cruel Intentions*
The image of Sarah Michelle Gellar teaching Selma Blair how to kiss in the park is etched into my brain for eternity. And I'm not cross about it.

Late 1990s–2000s HBO comedy *Sex and the City*
I still can't get over the episode where my favourite sex bomb Samantha Jones gets a girlfriend and declares, 'Yes ladies, I'm a lesbian.' My secretly homosexual mind is blown.

Computer game *The Sims*, which launched in 2000
As a teenager, I escape from reality by getting very into the life-simulation computer game. When I discover that female sims can 'woohoo' with each other, I get significantly more into it.

2000s BBC makeover show *What Not to Wear*
In the future I will understand why this programme is critiqued for its many problematic elements. But when I watch it live on TV at the time, all I can think about is how Trinny and Susannah keep grabbing each other's boobs.

Lucy Liu in the 2000 *Charlie's Angels* film
Specifically, the scene where Lucy wears a black leather dominatrix suit and cracks her whip as the soundtrack plays, 'Ooh, Barracuda. And I'm dead. See also: Lucy in 1990s TV show *Ally McBeal*, the episode where she snogs Calista Flockhart. Oh, basically see any time Lucy is on-screen in my youth. What can I say? I love Lucy Liu.

CHAPTER 2

I kissed a girl

Oh my god, this is really happening. Cassie is kissing me. Me. Muggins. The mug-meister. Being snogged senseless by a fit girl. Am I dreaming? Quite possibly, because this is batshit-bonkers. Can I pinch myself without destroying the vibe? I hope her parents don't come home early. Did she lock the . . . flipping heck, that feels good. Is this even legal? Probs not. This is way too much fun to be legal, but I'm here now. What's the saying? When in Rome . . . let Rome snog your face off?

The first time Cassie kisses me, it is without a doubt the most exciting thing that has ever happened in my life. Ok, so my day-to-day routine is hardly a nonstop rock 'n' roll thrill-fest. I don't get my kicks hooking up with groupies and chucking tellies out of hotel windows. I'm a thirteen-year-old lass from Leeds, not Jarvis bloody Cocker. The edgiest thing I've done to date is incur a library fine for an overdue *Baby-Sitters Club* book. By contrast, with her mischievous grin and penchant for innuendo, Cassie seems to promise adventure. In the context of my own mundane existence, the Cassie kiss is *wild*. It is Most Definitely Something.

It hasn't come completely out of the blue either. We've been building up to this watershed smooch for some time now.

I'm talking months of snuggling up at sleepovers while we watch romcoms about straight people falling in love. Cuddling turns into massages, turns into lengthy back rubs to Madonna's *Ray of Light* album, turns into this moment right now: this kiss. *The* kiss. The kiss of no return. The kiss that blows my world up. The kiss that changes everything.

We pull apart and look at each other. I feel nervous. She seems bold. Neither of us says anything. Our mouths meet again and it is soft, soft, soft. And slow. So slow. So this is how it starts. This is who we are when no one is watching.

It's the late 1990s and, like Tamagotchis and low-slung jeans with a little bit of thong peeping out, heterosexuality is every-where. We're in the age of Britpop and boy bands, lads and ladettes. Same-sex weddings won't be legal for another fifteen years, gay people are banned from the armed forces and the only real-life lesbian I've heard of is Sandi Toksvig. When the broadcaster came out four years before, in 1994, she received death threats so serious she had to go into hiding. The only place queerness exists in my life, it is safely locked away.

At thirteen years old I am, as far as anyone can tell, as poker straight as my hair, which is naturally curly but beaten into daily submission courtesy of my new Babyliss flat irons. SYMBOLIC. I wear train-track braces on my teeth. I have a paper round, a pink inflatable armchair and a pet tabby called Whisky. Whisky is one of my closest confidantes and certainly the male who knows me best. In a cruel twist of fate, I am a cat person with a severe allergy to cats, so ours is a love that brings me out in a rash. I will go on to find that relationships with men can have this effect on me. The rest of my skin is pale and blotchy but, excitingly, I have recently discovered fake tan and now my palms are an alarming shade of orange. As you can tell, I am extremely cool. Like every other teenage girl in the 1990s, I know all the words to 'Never Ever' by All

Saints and 'Let's Get Ready to Rhumble' by PJ & Duncan. I am low-key concerned about the Millennium Bug and extremely concerned that I am not thinner, prettier and less of a buffoon. And, also like every other teenage girl in the 1990s, ever since birth I have been indoctrinated by the patriarchy.

When other people are around, Cassie and I do what all the other girls do. We obsess about boys. When you're a teenage girl, boy-knowledge operates as social currency. Boys are the go-to conversation topic for rapid female bonding. Cassie and I are no exception as we perform the familiar rituals of girl-hood. We study magazines like *Sugar* and *Bliss*, memorizing tips on how to make a lad like you (two coats of Rimmel lip gloss, laugh at all his jokes). We play Dream Phone, a board game marketed to pre-teens where the objective is to sit by a fake fuchsia phone and literally wait for some guy to call. We compile lists of our top ten crushes. All of them are men, many are fictional: the tall one in Hanson who looks so cute when he 'MMMBops', the local paper delivery boy who we have never spoken to but who, this one time, waved at us, the male characters in the cartoon version of *Beauty and the Beast*. Cassie favours built-like-a-brick-shithouse Gaston, while I prefer the cheeky, non-threatening charms of Lumière, the talking candlestick.

Time passes, we survive Y2K and Operation Covert Lez Off is still going strong in the twenty-first century. Our clan-destine rendezvous, cunningly disguised as innocent slumber parties, are a regular occurrence. The only upside to the complete lack of gay representation in the media is that no one suspects a goddamn thing. We can hide in plain sight, no need for an alibi. If she was a he, we'd never be allowed this much unsupervised one-on-one time. Lesbian invisibility is our super-power and our kryptonite.

What do we get up to when we're alone? It isn't some porn

version of girl-on-girl action. It isn't sleazy or even particularly graphic. To me, it feels like being inside one of those pre-Raphaelite paintings of woodland nymphs cavorting in a pond, at one with nature, flowers in their flowing locks, their boobs bouncing freely in the breeze. Playful, silly, just what girls do, it's almost wholesome and it feels totally natural. We have bubble baths and cuddling marathons and unbridled giggling fits. We bask in the delicious sensuality of this feminine dreamland we have invented. Our romance is the lightest touch sparking the deepest tremor. It is the ancient erotic art of dry-humping. It is a caress that lasts an eternity. It is her lips and my lips and her lips and my lips ad infinitum.

In short, it is all so very gay. What isn't so very gay is the total lack of discussion, deconstruction and analysis. We don't talk about how we feel for each other or what any of this incessant frottage might mean. I don't interrogate it privately in my own head either. It feels safer not to go there. My body and my brain are out of sync. In the moments following a particularly intense heavy petting session, I whisper, 'Serious question. Who do you think is the fittest in Boyzone?' To speak the truth would break the spell. Saying it out loud would make this all too real, too dangerous. There would be no plausible deniability. If we don't talk about it, we could still technically claim we accidentally fell on top of each other, lips first. Just maybe if we keep this thing purely physical, if we never actually acknowledge it, our connection, this energy between us will exist in some other dimension, some dreamlike, ethereal state where we do not have to answer for our actions. Or maybe we never speak about it because we do not have the words.

The whole time I am secretly snogging my mate at any opportunity, I am also attending school under Section 28. This pernicious legislation, introduced in 1988 by the Conservative government, forbids local authorities and schools from 'the teaching of the acceptability of homosexuality as a pretended family relationship'.

The October before this hateful clause is enshrined in law, Prime Minister Margaret Thatcher gives a speech at the Tory party's annual conference. Dressed in a 1980s power skirt suit in periwinkle blue, complete with matching pussybow blouse, she declares, 'It's the plight of individual boys and girls that worries me most.' Sweet of you to care, Maggie. Do go on. 'Children, who need to be taught to respect traditional moral values, are being taught that they have an inalienable right to be gay. All of those children are being cheated of a sound start in life.'

How ironic that I, aged two at the time, will soon enter an education system designed to shame and silence my very nature. It is the first overtly anti-gay law to be introduced in the UK in a century and it is introduced the same year I start nursery. It won't be repealed until the year I leave sixth form. I can't help taking this personally. It is, at the very least, a highly suspicious timeline. Why is the government so keen for me in particular not to find out about homosexuality? Why all this effort to hide gay stuff from little old me? It begs the question, just how powerful is my lesbianism? Plot twist: am I, in fact, a mighty lezzy wizard who cannot discover her true nature lest I become too immense and take over the world? To be honest, that sounds pretty cool and like the premise of a film I would definitely watch. But while I'm at school, I do not think about any of this. I do not comprehend that throughout my entire education, I am being trained to hate what I am.

Section 28 means that queer is never mentioned. Queer is unspeakable. The education system is gaslighting me into believing I don't exist. Of course, I'm still young and know little of the law. I will not realize what is happening around me, what is happening *to me*, until much, much later. For now,

I do not grasp that in my place of learning, the place I go every day to prepare me for adulthood, it is literally illegal to say anything good about gay people.

Alongside French verb conjugation and Pythagoras' Theorem, I am taught to deny the fibre of my being. Internalized homophobia is part of the government-sanctioned curriculum and I am one diligent student. At the same time I am having it ingrained in me that queer is shameful and lesser and wrong, so are all the other queer students. And the straight students too. If I wasn't so incandescent with rage, I might marvel at the efficiency of a system that keeps marginalized people in our place, in school, in society, within our own selves.

❖

But let's not stay too riled up too long. Many years later I'm all grown up and I am standing inside Queer Britain, the UK's first dedicated bricks-and-mortar LGBTQIA museum. My eyes are wide, partly with wonder, partly because I'm trying really hard not to openly bawl in public. As usual, queer people have created the representation we desperately need to see that has been so woefully absent all our lives. Look over there! Awe-inspiring photographs of early gay rights protesters defiantly marching for our liberation. And there! Statues of groundbreaking lesbian activists, Lady Phyll and Christine Burns. Ohmygodwhatsthis? A vintage comic called *Dyke's Delight*?! This place is a feast for my senses and a balm for my wounded heart.

So we've come a long way, right? We have Queer Britain and LGBT+ History Month to celebrate our rich past, and organizations like LGBTQIA anti-bullying charity Diversity Role Models and LGBTQIA youth charity Just Like Us to teach present-day students that it's ok to be different. Improvements have indeed been made, but we cannot afford to take that progress for granted.

As I write these words, there are disturbing signs that we are sliding backwards fast. The parallels between Section 28 and the 'Don't Say Gay' bill in the US are obvious and chilling. This new law passed in Florida in 2022, prohibiting 'classroom discussion about sexual orientation or gender identity in certain grade levels'. Sound familiar? Then there's the pushback here in the UK, with queer and trans books being removed from children's museums, like when in 2023 the V&A's Children's Centre removed two trans-affirming books and a poster that read 'Some people are trans. Get over it!' There is also the worrying rise in parents protesting outside schools, brandishing homemade banners proclaiming 'Let kids be kids'. I'm talking about protests like the demonstration against LGBTQIA equality lessons that took place outside a primary school in Birmingham in 2019. It was later ruled by a high court judge that these protesting parents had 'grossly misrepresented' what was actually being taught to children.

Which begs the question, what exactly do these parents think is going on in those lessons? 'So class, today we're going to make our own strap-ons! I hope you all remembered your belts, big pants and cucumbers.' Norma, chill your boots and step away from the banner. That is not something you need to be worried about happening. And still they cry out, 'Let kids be kids'. Let's think about that for a second. What about the gay, bi and trans kids? Statistically it's pretty likely there are some in that classroom. And what about the kids with queer parents or relatives or friends? What about the kids who live in a world where LGBTQIA people exist, i.e. *all* of the kids? And too much of what exactly? Too much useful, age-appropriate information about reality? Sorry to break this to you, Norma, but while LGBTQIA people may seem special and magical like unicorns, it is a proven fact that we are real. While we're on the subject of fairytale beings, children are always reading storybooks about princesses going round kissing frogs, right? So bestiality is A-ok, but don't dare mention that some children have two daddies? If the whole 'telling kids about gay people turns them gay' notion was true, then the world would be full of grown adults puckering up for amphibians. Stop this madness!

Withholding information about queer identities does not prevent kids from being queer. All it does is actively harm the ones who are, as well as those who come from queer families, and wilfully mislead everyone else. In the absence of positive education, misinformation and prejudice abounds. Homophobic bullying happens. Trans suicide happens. The queer kids get the message loud and clear: we are not valid, we are not welcome, we are not safe. And we aren't the ones hurting anyone. We are the ones being hurt by a climate of erasure that fears and others us. If we were taught that queer people could do wonderful things, hell if we were taught that queer people could even just *be*, it would save so many lives.

When I look back at my adolescence, I remember those thrilling secret snogging sessions and I think, 'Good on you, girl'. But I also remember so much shame. The vacuum where positive representation and inclusive information should have been was filled instead with government-endorsed self-loathing. How different would my schooldays have been if queer identities weren't at best erased, at worst demonized? I'm not saying I would have proudly stood in my truth and declared my homosexuality to the world aged thirteen. But it might have made me feel safe to at least think about this stuff in my own head. You see, it wasn't just that it didn't feel safe for me to come out to other people. It didn't feel safe for me to even come out to myself, to consider for just a second the very real possibility that I might not be so straight after all.

Things I hear when
I'm a teenage girl

Tits!

Big tits!

Show us your big tits!

Oi, oi!

Have you got a boyfriend?

Can I have your number?

What's your problem?

Frigid.

Slag.

Don't be such a prick-tease.

Don't be such a prude.

Ugly cow.

Fat cow.

Moo.

You can't wear that. You look like you're asking for it.

You can't wear that. You look like a sack of tatties.

Men love it when you laugh at their jokes.

Stop laughing so loud.

Everyone knows women aren't funny.

Stop showing off.

You're embarrassing yourself.

Give us a smile, love.

What are you smiling at?

You can't trust men. They're only after one thing.

You can't trust women. They bitch about you behind your back.

It is really important for a woman to be as good-looking as possible.

There is nothing more attractive than a woman who doesn't realize how good-looking she is.

Lesbians are ugly and wear sensible shoes.

Lesbians are just women who can't get a man.

Lesbians are perverts.

Weirdo.

Do better.

Try harder.

Stop trying so hard.

Who do you think you are?

You are not enough.

You are way too much.

Things I never hear when I'm a teenage girl

Lesbians exist and if you are one, that's ok.

CHAPTER 3

A bit about boys and girls

The world I grow up in is obsessed with boys and girls. I can only really relate to the being obsessed with girls part. Yet despite my devotion to my own gender, when I turn eleven and start going to an all-girls high school, I do not love it. The reason for this has a bit to do with boys and a lot to do with money.

After attending my local state primary school, at my mum's urging I sit the entrance exams and undergo the interview process to apply to private school for secondary school. I am awarded an academic scholarship and my mum is overjoyed.

In theory, attending an all-girls school should be halcyon days for me, a girl who secretly loves girls. But in practice, somehow it isn't. I never quite manage to shake the inkling that I do not belong in this 'elite' establishment, that although my family isn't below the breadline we are nowhere near rich enough, that our house isn't fancy enough, that I am simply not of this cosseted, closed-off realm. Even the uniform list of items each pupil must acquire before term starts is mind-boggling. It's like something from an Enid Blyton book. There is an actual jolly hockey stick.

From day one, I am acutely aware that, despite the fact we are all wearing the same regulation shade of bottle-green tartan, I don't fit in with the other girls. We are hoarded into a high-ceilinged, dustily grand assembly room. The teacher shushes us into silence, but a charge lingers in the air. It's a sort of high-frequency, communal electricity and it unnerves me greatly. This cavernous room is packed with unfamiliar girls in green, many of whom have known each other since they were three. Looking around, I can't help thinking of that bit in Roald Dahl's *The Witches*, when the witches have their annual meeting to plot the extermination of all children. A bookworm almost since birth, I love Roald Dahl and arrogantly fancy myself as a bit of a Matilda figure. But I have always found this particular chapter to be the most harrowing thing imaginable.

I will never forget going to see the film adaptation. I am only four years old when it comes out. Sitting on the front row, I gaze up at the enormous screen, transfixed. I love The Grand High Witch. She's so confident and glamorous. Her hair is so shiny and just look at all that glittering jewellery. But then something awful happens. She is addressing an audience of women who, it transpires, are really witches in disguise. There is this strange, fizzing, ominous energy among them. Then The Grand High Witch theatrically peels off her wig and, horrifyingly, her whole face, revealing her real, gruesome, 'worm-eaten' visage. I am so petrified I start screaming incoherently and do not stop until I am forcibly removed from the screening.

This is one of my earliest memories. Perhaps it is the terror of this moment that jolts my whole memory system into being. And this is the memory I can't shake from my mind on my first day at high school. Of course, it's normal to be nervous when starting a new school and I'm not for a second suggesting that my classmates or teachers are in any way sinister. This isn't about them, it's about how I feel in this environment.

Unsettled, a misfit, ill at ease. The fish-out-of-water sensation does not subside over the following years. And this is without any added stigma of being out.

Oddly, being at an all-girls school seems to imbue the student body with a strange wariness about the danger of being stereotyped as lesbians. It becomes a sort of self-conscious school joke. One day, we are on a geography field trip. After the excitement of clambering aboard a coach and being allowed for this special occasion to wear non-regulation coats, we are boisterous, we are pubescent, we are girls on tour. Rambling along a countryside path, buoyed up by fresh air and the illusion of freedom, a singalong strikes up. Our anthem? Not the school song, which is all in Latin and rather gloomy, but our own spin on a classic campfire tune.

'Everywhere we go / People always ask us / Who we are / Where we come from / So we tell them / We're from Leeds Girls' High School / And they ask us / Are we all lesbians?'

Cue mass hysteria. This is clearly the funniest thing anyone has ever said, let alone sung. Lesbian is perennially the punchline, the most hilarious gag imaginable, certainly not something I could ever feel ok about being.

The other thing about this all-girls school is that boys, in their absence, are elevated to godlike status. They are placed on the highest pedestal. Proximity to boys from the boys' school equals social power, and rivalry for male attention is rife and toxic. Boys are what we talk about the most. We can gossip about boys all day long and I am onboard, as long as the boys remain an abstract concept. Being face-to-face with them is a different matter.

❉

I am at an under-eighteens night at a club called Evolution. Ironically, courtship rituals in this establishment are far from evolved. I've already had my bum groped, my boobs grabbed and my crotch squeezed by three separate strangers, but I'm a girl so this is pretty much unavoidable unless I never leave the house again. Unwanted attention from men is par for the course. Pervy blokes driving white vans and swarms of lads swaggering down the street have been bellowing 'tits' at me for years now. One time, a crowd of teenage boys blocks my path so I have to walk through them and as I do, I hear whispering from every angle, in menacing unison: 'Tits, tits, tits.' At the time I go home and weep, but later on I can't help marvelling at their coordinated vocal harmony, like a spoken-word choir of chauvinist wankers.

Sidenote: do these men think they're telling me something I haven't already noticed? Are they expecting me to look down and be flabbergasted by what I see? 'Oh my god, where did these come from? And will you please go out with me, you observant stallion?!' I daydream about starting a construction company where builders shout feminist affirmations at women: 'Cor! Look at her massive set . . . of original ideas and valid opinions!' In all seriousness, every time I am catcalled it makes my cheeks go red, my body tense up and my voice wither into silence with shame, but it's also, I think to myself at the time, just what happens to women.

Let's get back to this night. So I'm sat chatting to a guy with spiky hair, which looks all hard and shiny with gel. To be more accurate, he is doing most of the chat-shouting over the blasting din of the music ('We like to Party (The Vengabus)' by Vengaboys). I am nodding along encouragingly. He is drenched in Lynx, dressed all in black and looks vaguely pop-punk, like he probably listens to a lot of Blink-182, which seems impressively counter-culture. I wear Impulse body spray and an outfit I bought from the Miss Selfridge sale rack with money I saved from my Saturday job. He talks at length about bands I've never heard of. I pretend to know who they are. Strategically, I do not mention my abiding love of the Spice Girls and how devastated I still am about Geri leaving.

I have never kissed a boy before and tonight might be the night. After all, my friends have started kissing boys. Cassie has started kissing boys. I should probably give this whole kissing boys thing a whirl or risk being labelled 'frigid' for life. Could pop-punk, hard-hair guy be the one? There's no time to consider this further, because now he's lunging directly towards me. His eyes are closing. His lips are scrunching up. Here we go. It's on.

Come on, Rox. YOU'VE GOT THIS! What would Ginger do? She'd spice up her life, that's what! Girl power. Let's do this. Deep breath. Ok. I'm channelling Ginge. I'm closing my eyes. I'm scrunching my lips. I'm – no. Nonononono. That's a no from me.

Pure panic and my body takes over. In an automatic self-defence reflex, I curl myself up into a human ball like Sonic the fucking Hedgehog. It doesn't hurt his feelings, because he just thinks I'm insane.

It would be convenient to say that I know for sure I'm gay in this moment, that I have put together the two blindingly obvious matching jigsaw pieces and worked out that I'm a whopping great lezatron. But I don't know that yet. Hang on, that's not quite right. My body knows something's up. My horny, betraying body craves the pleasure only another woman can give it. It vehemently rejects the idea of intimacy with a man. But my rational mind?

Don't think about it. Put it in a box, shut the lid and throw away the key.

I do know this much. I do know that I am much more interested in spending time in the world of women. Boys are fine as a means to bond with female friends, but I am so much more fascinated by girls. I am gripped by female-created art and female-centric stories. Strong, creative, vibrant women captivate me. And I know that I find most men at best a bit dull, at worst a visceral threat. But all that can be explained away by feminism, right? So no soul-searching occurs.

Not about that anyway. But like all teenagers throughout history, I am consumed with the gargantuan task of discovering and constructing who I am, at the same time as I am understanding, often in blunt and brutal fashion, how the world sees me. No matter what sexuality you are, being a teenage girl is, to put it politely, a monumental headfuck. I am constantly being told who I am, but there is a disconnect between my private self and other people's perception of me. The one label they never call me is the one label that is true. Nobody knows I'm a lesbian. How could they? I don't even know. I am a stranger to myself.

❉

What's it like the first time I actually kiss a boy? In one word: dull. It eventually happens on an escalator in a shopping centre in broad daylight. This is what constitutes a romantic date in my teenage world. I've been refusing to kiss this boy for some time now. I'm starting to worry I'm being terribly rude. We met during a joint production between the boys' and girls' schools of Shakespeare's *A Midsummer Night's Dream*. I am playing – talk about typecasting – Titania. Yes, TIT-ania. Hey, it's a great part. I am delighted to channel the fairy queen who falls in love with a man called Bottom who has an ass for a head. Comedy, glamour, plenty of long, show-offy speeches: what's not to love? But the casting of me and my knockers in this role is naturally the cause of much mirth among the boys. Escalator guy is playing either Lysander or Demetrius. I'm pretty rubbish at telling straight men apart, even now. Anyway, Lysanderordemetrius has let it be known among the local community, by which I mean the cast of this play and the A-listers at school who are cool enough to have connections with boys, that he wants to 'pull' me.

In late-nineties/early-noughties Leeds private school vernacular, courtship rituals are described by brisk verbs and unseductive nouns. 'Pulling' equals snogging. Then there's 'tossing off', i.e. administering a hand job. The 'tit wank' is a popular craze that sounds frankly terrifying. There's also a lot of talk about 'topping'. Now in this context 'topping' does not mean what it will mean in the future when I start having queer adventures in the sack (we'll get to that later). Here 'topping' means simply 'the groping of tits'. Groping might be too gentle a word for it. More often than not, it is more like furious kneading. Due to my hefty bosoms, quite a few of the boys at the boys' school have expressed their interest in 'topping' me. One of these boys is Lysanderordemetrius.

At a recent house party, he was so frustrated I wouldn't lock lips and offer up my jugs for his pleasure that he punched a hole in the wall. The weirdest part was that everyone acted like this was a huge compliment. I thought it was a bit much and extremely rude to the party host's poor parents, who came home to discover their property had been vandalized. Seriously, Lysanderordemetrius, just find someone else to pull and top! But he wanted to specifically pull and top me. I had been chosen, which sounds like I'm boasting. I'm not, because it had been made very clear to me that Lysanderordemetrius had only chosen me because of my aforementioned massive honkers.

Throughout my adolescence I am repeatedly made aware that my worth, by which I mean my desirability, is tied up solely in my body. I am often reminded that I am only ever fancied because of my figure, never my face or, god forbid, my personality. A popular girl in my year, let's call her Regina, as in George, as in *Mean Girls*, tells me witheringly, 'Lysanderordemetrius said he wants to pull you, but you do know it's just because of your boobs, yeah? Like Lysanderordemetrius is really into your boobs. He told me, because . . . (*a smug giggle*) . . . we're kind of close . . . Lysanderordemetrius told me his ideal girl would have your boobs, but with like, Amanda's face. Like your boobs are a ten and your face is a five. Maybe a six with make-up.' How could I not be wooed by such flattery?! God, being a teenager is brutal, a minefield of mortification.

So here we are, on an escalator in the centre of Leeds. I'm not sure why he goes for it while we're on a moving stairway. Maybe we've run out of things to talk about. Perhaps he thinks it's cinematic. Feeling extremely self-conscious, I keep my eyes open throughout.

I've got to do this. I've got to get this done. If Titania can snog a man with a donkey's face, then I can snog this guy. His face is human. It's not a bad face. Slightly sleazy smile, but nice eyes. Ok, so they're permanently fixated on my chest but that's probably my fault somehow. Here we go! I'm doing pulling. I'm being pulled . . .

Oh wow . . .

This is . . .

very . . .

very . . .

boring.

Yes, that's the word. I'm having my first kiss with a boy on an escalator and people are staring and I am bored! Oops, bit sloppy. How long do we have to keep doing this?

Oh great, we're nearly at the end of the escalator. We can stop now and just go back to him ogling my boobs.

And so, I kiss him. Or more accurately, I let him kiss me. But of course, his kiss cannot compare to Cassie's.

❊

At the age of sixteen I decide to leave the private school system for good. I strongly feel that it isn't the real world and it isn't the right place for me. Despite how much I love girls, I've never felt I belonged. I didn't on day one and I still don't five years later. In a surprising turn of events I, a closeted lesbian agnostic, choose to transfer from my all-girls school to a comprehensive, co-ed, Catholic sixth form college.

It's my first day at my new college and I've just taken a seat for assembly. I'm looking around at all my fellow students. Then I notice one girl in particular. A petite strawberry blonde in a sunshine-hued top. She doesn't walk, she struts with theatrical flair, her face expressive and captivating. Among this flock of cookie-cutter students with their matching jeans, highlights and bored expressions, she stands out like a bird of paradise. I do not fancy her. This is not a lust-at-first-sight moment. What I'm feeling is very different indeed.

Newsflash: queer women don't automatically fancy every woman we meet. In fact, that is a homophobic myth, probably designed to make straight women scared of us. The reality is that of course we can have wonderful platonic relationships with women, and that is what I want with this charismatic vision in yellow. I look at this vivid, vibrant girl and I really, really want to be her friend. She just seems so fabulous! I want to be around that energy.

I meet Lela formally, predictably, when we both audition for the college play. The show is Greek tragedy, *The Bacchae*. I score the part of Agave, the ringleader of a sex-crazed cult of drugged-up women who worship Bacchus, The God of Pleasure. Lela is cast in a plum role in the tribe and we get on immediately. Bonding in rehearsals, we quickly become close. We have so much in common. We both obsess over old Hollywood movie stars, dance with our whole hearts and are invariably the two most dressed-up people in any classroom.

One day we are walking arm in arm through Leeds city centre, on one of our many shopping expeditions. We're chatting away, frequently dissolving into giggles and revelling in our newfound friendship. Glancing around, I notice that strangers are staring. This is nothing new. Strangers have always stared at me. They've often sniggered too, whether because of my comedically outsize bosoms, my thrift store get-up or my too-loud guffawing I've forgotten to rein in. For as long as I can remember, it's made me feel extraordinarily uncomfortable. But today the pedestrians aren't just gawping at me. They're gawping at Lela too, at her striking beauty, unique style and carefree laughter.

I think about what I thought the first time I saw her, that she looked fun and special and I really wanted to be her friend. Then I look at her to see how she's coping with the stares. And I see that she doesn't let them shake her. She carries on being her gorgeous, authentic self.

Something crystallizes for me in this moment. My whole perspective shifts. An epiphany takes place outside The Merrion shopping centre. I am hit with the realization that standing out from the herd is something to be cherished. I know without a doubt that Lela is awesome. And if someone as awesome as her wants to be my friend, it figures that I can't be so bad myself. It gives me confidence, this realization. It makes me care less about what strangers think of me. It gifts me with a new determination to be my whole self to the hilt. Let them stare. I'm too busy living in the moment with my incredible friend.

I love my new college. I feel so much freer and more grown

up than I did at school. I'm meeting new people and making new friends and only studying subjects I'm passionate about: English, Theatre and French. I work hard and throw myself into extracurricular activities like the geek I've always been. Between revising for exams, editing the college paper and performing in all the plays, my diary is conveniently full. This leaves absolutely no time for pursuing romance of any kind. It's almost as if I'm keeping myself so busy there isn't a spare moment to face dealing with a love life.

By this time Cassie and I have drifted apart. Our once-frantic, frequent rendezvous have fizzled away to nothing and now we don't really talk much any more. Just as we never spoke about the kisses we shared, we don't address their absence either. Although I loved what we did together and although I have love for her, I am not and never have been in love with Cassie. I was always more thrilled by her than enamoured. It was more about physical sensation than emotional interrogation. Experimentation feels too clinical a word to describe what we were to each other. We were young. We were just doing what felt natural for us. We were close friends with queer investigative benefits. Despite our years of illicit encounters, Cassie and I never progressed beyond canoodling. We never had sex of any kind and I have done no more than been 'pulled' and 'topped' by boys. For those two years at college, people repeatedly assume I am a maneater, when in truth I am celibate. I don't date anyone of any gender, in the open or in private.

(True) entries from my teenage diary, aged seventeen and eighteen

Dear diary,
College is great. Made loads of mates. I think some people don't know what to make of me because I'm so individual. But it's like Destiny's Child sings in my current motivational theme song, 'Happy Face': sure, there are lots of people who don't like me, but loads more who love me and I love myself.

Dez keeps dropping hints that he's into me. He told all our mutual friends that he fancies me. This is an ego boost, but it's not going anywhere. He did say I have a nice ass. I'm so used to tits-this and tits-that, I'm always secretly a little bit flattered when my ass finally gets some airtime.

Anyway, he's too experienced. Player material. Just out of a year-long relationship (which, worryingly, broke up a week after I met him). If I were to go out with him – IF – then he'd want to have all the sex and see me naked and do the rude stuff that he takes for granted when he's got a girlfriend. I know I'm seventeen, but I'm not sure I'm ready for any of that.

Also, I wouldn't want to disappoint him. That sounds really bad. I know it should be about my pleasure too. But what if he didn't fancy me naked? What if I wasn't good enough? I don't like doing things I'm not good at. I'm so glad I don't have to do P.E. any more.

Dear diary,
I think I may, as Lysanderordemetrius once put it, 'ooze sex from every pore'. Don't worry, diary, there is no leakage!

According to people at college I talk like a porn star (entirely unintentional) and would make a fantastic 'lesbinim'.

I was just chatting to Mel on MSN Messenger about never finding people who fancy me that I fancy back. This is what she wrote.

Mel says:
loads of people fancy u

A sweet lie from Mel. They <u>definitely</u> don't. But then she wrote this.

Mel says:
. . . i do

IS SHE JOKING?
IS SHE BEING SERIOUS?
I HONESTLY CAN'T TELL!!!
Mel is bisexual. She lost her virginity to a boy at fifteen and to a girl at fourteen.

I get nervous around her. We do this sort of joke-flirting thing and I can't tell if either of us means it.

Dear diary,
Interrailing around Europe with Lela. We're broke so we're staying in hostels and raiding the breakfast buffet to survive each day. Last night we slept on the beach in Nice, so we could use the money we saved to treat ourselves to one evening in a hotel.

We stayed up talking late into the night. We were both staring up into the pitch-black sky and completely out of the blue I asked her, 'Lela, do you masturbate?'

She told me that in that moment she knew we could talk

to each other about absolutely anything. *How lucky am I to have such a close female friend?*

Eventually we drifted off to sleep, using our backpacks as pillows. Then at dawn, I suddenly became aware of a jet of water spraying in my face. 'Beach police!' I yelled in panic. 'Wake up, Lela! The beach police are after us!'

Flustered and drowsy, we bundled our belongings up in our arms and made a dash for it. Turns out they have special boats that patrol the coastline spraying water to keep the beach clean. Who knew? The French sure know how to live.

Can't wait to sleep in a proper bed tonight.

CHAPTER 4

Experimenting with heterosexuality

It's 2004, I'm nineteen and my bedroom is full of naked women. Sadly, I'm not hosting a sapphic orgy. Instead, after watching countless hours of interiors TV show *Changing Rooms*, I have created my very own feature wall and plastered every inch of it with tasteful black and white photographs of diverse babes in the buff. There are women with cascading manes and women with shaved heads. There are sinewy gym bunnies and voluptuous goddesses. There are stretch marks and beaming smiles and six packs and tummy rolls and tattoos and body hair and full bushes. Every single one of these women is a work of art. They're all spectacular and they're all starkers. Behold, my Great Wall of Vagina.

My extensive private collection of nudes should be a clue to something significant, but I'm not picking up on that. What? Could my literal shrine to naked women be a subtle manifestation of repressed homosexuality? Pah! Surely not. The reason I have this collage of bombshells in their birthday suits is because I am a feminist. In fact, I am such a committed and strident feminist that right now I'm performing in an amateur street theatre production of *The Vagina Monologues*. I can't deny, this is very on brand.

At this point in my life, I am at uni in Manchester studying drama. My spare time is spent pounding the city's rain-sodden pavements alongside a small group of like-minded vulva-owners, shouting this sort of thing at strangers, *voluntarily*: 'The clitoris is the only organ in the body designed purely for pleasure!' 'Pussies unite!' 'VAGINA MOTHERFUCKERS!'

It's a choral piece, but I do have a solo, which I'm very excited about. My star turn is a rousing rendition of a mono-logue entitled 'Because He Liked to Look at It'. The audience reviews are, I'll admit, mixed. Some bystanders are deeply offended, others thoroughly tickled. A few show solidarity by raising their fists and, I'm sure in spirit, their vaginas. Quite a lot of onlookers just seem really confused, but my favourites have to be the ones who casually stroll on by barely giving us a second glance. We may be mouthing off about our muffs, but that does not faze them. They have an aura that seems to say, 'Ah yes, the Mad Vagina Ladies. You're here every weekday, aren't you? Well, carry on cunting. I've got to get to Boots before it closes.'

I come into possession of my full-frontal photo stash one day in the rehearsal room. Our director fans the photocopied images out across the floor, prompting an emotional group discussion about body image. Feeling empowered and inex-plicably horny, I take the pics back to my digs and embark on the most homoerotic home décor project ever. But I honestly don't see it like that. I don't twig what all those titties are trying to tell me. I genuinely believe that by displaying an abundance of nipples and noonies, I am simply *doing* feminism. I am doing body positivity, celebrating the diverse glory of my magnificent gender. And I am most certainly not lingering my gaze a few seconds too long on that sporty one with the knowing grin. When friends come round and notice the gallery of gash, which in fairness to them is pretty difficult to miss, they ask with one eyebrow raised, 'What's all this about then?'

'This,' I reply rather grandly, 'is my Feminist Art. Now, let me tell you some facts I recently learned about vaginas.'

One student director sees my potential to be convincing as a massive gay and casts me as Inez, the lesbian in Jean Paul Sartre's existential masterpiece, *No Exit*. He takes one look at me and decides, 'Hmm, she could be a homosexual.' I, on the other hand, am no closer to that realization. Landing this part means I get to roleplay being gay, which should be wonderful and help me work through some stuff, and it is and it does, but it's also kind of horrifying. *No Exit* is a three-hander about being trapped in hell for eternity as punishment for your terrible deeds on Earth. Inez's crime? Being gay and killing people. So this is another of my formative representations of lesbianism. A friend from my course is in a different play called *Rope*. Thrillingly, it's about two gay men. Dispiritingly, they are both sadistic murderers. Jeez, this is *Bad Girls* all over again, only this time I'm stuck in a draughty black box studio theatre and I can't change the channel.

When I'm not pretending to be a lesbian onstage, pretending not to be a lesbian in real life or yelling 'cunt' at confused pedestrians in an attempt to empower them, I can be found binge-watching *The Sopranos* with my boyfriend. Yes, at nineteen I finally bag myself my first boyfriend. To the outside world, I am living my best straight life.

In my first year, I live in halls of residence in a flat share with seven other women. Across the hallway is a corresponding flat containing eight guys. Liam is the nicest of the closest available men. He is sweet, funny and enthusiastic about Manchester United, Oasis and boobs. On paper he's your quintessential lad, the target reader of *Nuts* magazine, but in person he is much more than a two-dimensional stereotype. He's gentle and kind with a cheeky grin. We have nothing in common (apart from our fondness for funbags), but I genuinely really enjoy spending time with him. I like our companionship. I like our jokey repartee. I like the novelty of finally having a boyfriend after all my years of singledom. I am trying heterosexuality out for size and I couldn't have picked a nicer bloke to give being straight a shot with.

He is the first and one of the very few men I ever sleep with. After months of being an item, we finally decide to do it. I am as ready as I will ever be. I care about Liam. Crucially, I feel safe with him, perhaps safer than I have ever felt with any man. Virginity is a very big deal in these days. Culturally, it is imbued with huge significance, positioned as a rite of passage and a plot device in pretty much every American high school movie I grew up watching.

As I wake up on our designated V-day, I think to myself, 'By the time I go to sleep tonight, I will no longer be a virgin. This is a pivotal day in my life as a woman.' Always one to embrace a theme, I choose my outfit with a theatrical sense of symbolism. I settle on a flowing white summer dress, which is faintly bridal and extremely on the nose. This is what happens when you spend too much time studying drama. We have planned today's itinerary in detail, discussing contraception, making sure we both feel totally ready, choosing exactly when and where we will do the deed. We do it in my single bed in my small room. It hurts, but I was expecting that. I don't reach exhilarating heights of erotic pleasure, but I was expecting that too.

Later on, I will view the whole concept of virginity differently. I will realize that it is a social construct. My understanding of what constitutes sex will change as well. It will expand beyond the traditional definition of heterosexual intercourse and my life will be all the better for it. But I'd be lying if I said I had that all figured out already in this moment here.

Afterwards, Liam wraps his arms around me, we lie together and I feel close to him. We have seen each other and held each other through this intimate act. Of all the men in all the world, I am relieved I did this with him. A good, sweet man with kind eyes who makes me laugh. I don't feel fundamentally altered after the fact. I haven't suddenly become a woman. But I have had a new experience, an experience I have been taught to believe is defining.

There's no need for me to go into further details about my sex life with Liam. That's between me and – oh, alright then. There is one other time which seems significant. It's the middle of the day, but we're hanging out at mine. Neither of us has lectures and I'm not due to trot off and shout 'vagina' at strangers for another few hours. We start kissing, which inevitably leads to more than kissing. This is nothing groundbreaking. But what's different on this occasion is that we try something new. We attempt to spice things up, by experimenting with some extremely amateur dirty talk.

A complete novice in the dirty talk arena, I am self-conscious and stilted. With no game whatsoever I nervously stammer short, not-remotely-dirty phrases: 'You like that?' 'Oh, yeah baby' and a feeble, 'That's hot.'

I am grasping for something to say that might make this less cringeworthy. Then inspiration strikes. How do I finally get into the mood? What scenario turns out to be quite the aphrodisiac? Why, talking about me getting it on with another girl, of course. And so we copulate, egged on by me narrating my secret sapphic fantasies, under the watchful gaze of my Great Wall of Vagina. Read the signs, Rox!!

For two cosy years, Liam and I eat takeaway pizzas and play video games and cuddle up together and it is all very pleasant. There is nothing wrong with him, nothing obviously wrong with us. We really get on, rarely argue and have a great laugh. I would go so far as to say I love him, and yet . . . something niggles. Something is not quite right. There is a restlessness twitching deep within me, a yearning that is becoming harder to suppress. We really are so good together. As friends.

There is an alternate reality version of my life where I end up with Liam, or a man like him, a Liamalike. On this existential plane I meet a nice, non-threatening guy and together we carve out a life. Maybe we get married. Perhaps we have kids. I ask myself so many times if I could be happy with that existence, if I could be content or at least content *enough*. The problem is that if I'm being honest with myself, deep down, I know I couldn't. I know that this gnawing, longing feeling would never totally disappear and that it would be unfair on both of us to stay in that particular comforting half-truth. This is no judgement on women who do. I get it. I could so easily have done that myself. In some ways, it would have made things a whole lot simpler.

So why do I go out with a man for two years when there have been so many signs for so long that I am very much into women? Because my entire life has been spent in a society where heterosexuality is the default. Because pursuing a relationship with a woman is never presented as a viable option. Because having a boyfriend is what is expected. Because marrying a man is viewed as a woman's major accomplishment. Because I have resisted being with a man for this long and surely I'll have to do it eventually. Because he really is lovely and maybe that's enough to make this work. Because if I try with all my might, perhaps I can will myself to be content with this good, kind man, and maybe that will save people I love from pain.

Untangling how you've been conditioned to behave and view yourself from your actual instincts and authentic desires is a confusing, complicated business. Separating what I've been told I want from what I actually want is not as easy as it sounds. In so many ways, my identity, including how the world sees me and, to an extent, how I see myself, has been defined in relation to men.

There's a term for this: compulsory heterosexuality. It is explored in detail in Adrienne Rich's 1980 essay, 'Compulsory Heterosexuality and Lesbian Existence', and again in Angeli Luz's 'Lesbian Masterdoc'. When the thirty-page Google Doc goes viral in 2022, it quickly becomes canon for thousands of women struggling to fully understand their sexual identity because, like me, they have grown up in a world built around the assumption that everyone is straight.

As for the passion, I like Liam as a person, so I can find being fancied by him flattering. My vanity gets validated. I experience a certain amount of enjoyment from watching how he looks at me, the way my ego imagines I appear in his eyes. And truthfully, I do take satisfaction in making him feel good. What can I say? If I'm going to do something, I like to do it well. And I care about Liam. Of course I want him to be happy.

Still, our relationship does not last. I tell him I will always care about him, but something is 'not quite right' and it's best we go our separate ways. As far as break-ups go, this one is very amicable. Like I said, lovely guy.

Newly single, I begin tentatively connecting with queerness. I still don't know any actual out lesbians, but I have met Dylan, a Welsh dreamboat who shares my passion for power ballads and pop divas who go by their first name. Cher, Kylie, Madonna, we pull shapes and lip-sync for our lives to all the greats. With Dylan, I can be my silliest, campest self. He is my first openly queer close friend and I utterly adore him.

Dylan introduces me to gay male culture and the pure pleasure of a queer dance partner who really gets you. We trip the light fantastic at clubs, house parties and illegal warehouse raves. If no dancefloor is readily available, we don't let that hold us back. Hours evaporate in my room, while we improvise extensive interpretive dance duets to 'Like a Prayer' for an audience of none. Well, none except for the dozens of naked women who still adorn my wall and watch on as we vogue to the disco beat.

A short story about
a wild night out

The music is pumping, the place is heaving and everyone has the biggest smiles on their faces. These people are so friendly! Just look at all these lovely people having a lovely time.

Tonight, Dylan and I are out with a group of mates in Sankeys, a staple of the Manchester rave scene. I have just taken a pill for the first time. One tiny little tablet and then the waves start coming, bringing me up, up, up and . . .

Now I am in ecstasy. Despite the risks, I wasn't nervous about taking it. Maybe because I'm too young to understand I'm not immortal, maybe because friends have done it before and they tell me it's amazing and no big deal, maybe because I long to forget the pain of life and just feel free. Right now, so far away from my hometown and the girl I have been, I am ravenous for new experiences. I crave novelty. I want to taste life, not just study it. I am experimenting with hetero-sexuality and Class As, and tonight Class As are winning.

Once uni is over, I won't take drugs much at all. When the party stops being fun and the comedowns start to scare me, I will back away from the substances and I won't miss them. But tonight is my first time on pills and I have never felt more euphoric.

I look at Dylan. I love this guy so much. I look around the venue and realize I love everyone here. Heck, I love everyone in the world. I am love and empathy and the liberated spirit of dance personified in one gurning woman with pupils the size of saucers. Conforming to all the cliches of someone's first time on E, I'm convinced I've just unlocked the secret to the world and the secret is love, baby.

With all my senses heightened by the chemicals rushing through my body, simple human touch feels exquisite. I'm cuddling my friends, getting my back stroked by strangers and talking absolute codswallop to randoms I will never see again but right now feel like my best buds. All my insecurities have melted away and I'm floating on a glittering sea of togetherness.

I meet a stunning woman with short hair and within sixty seconds I strongly suspect we are soulmates.

Is she flirting with me? She's magnificent. Let's snuggle!

We're caressing each other's skin and we're gazing into each other's eyes and before I know it, we're kissing. Surely this is the softest, sweetest, most sensual kiss that's ever been kissed.

Mmm, this feels soooo good. Short-haired Soulmate, I think I'm in love with you.

The next day, mouth dry and jaw aching, I have a flashback to that encounter with my short-haired, short-lived soulmate. But it can all be conveniently explained away as a side effect of me being high as a kite.

Wait, was that . . . something? No, don't be ridiculous. I wanted to snog everyone. I was just off my tits.

CHAPTER 5

Talking, laughing, loving, breathing, fighting, fucking

I tell nobody, not even Dylan, about the new crush that is consuming me. Her name is Kiara and I swear, when we're together it's like the air is throbbing. I'm honestly not sure what it means at first. I am *that* naïve. She is gorgeous. Ebony hair and dark, intense eyes. We laugh the whole time, but there's also this feeling, an unfamiliar forcefield that fills up whatever room we're in.

Then one day I'm hanging out at hers. We are sat on the bed together while I style her hair. As always, there is an energy between us, a crackling, confusing attraction. We go quiet for a moment and then she says suddenly, 'Can you feel it?' We both laugh, nervously, self-consciously. This feels absurd, dangerous, exciting. She leans in towards me, then stops herself abruptly and says incredulously, 'Oh my god, I was going to kiss you.' When I finish doing her hair she asks if I want her to do mine and this sounds crazy, but it feels almost like a sexual invitation. I'm so overwhelmed I make an excuse to leave.

The next time we see each other the electricity is still in the air. We laugh, then we freeze. 'Can you still feel it?' I ask.

'Yes,' she says. Then she suggests we get together the

following night and talk about what's going on, because we can't carry on like this.

When she comes over, my nervousness is ricocheting around my room. We knock back a three-quid bottle of Australian red from the corner shop at breakneck speed. I genuinely believe that our appointment is to discuss how we're going to alleviate the tension between us. But I am hammered and she is gorgeous and suddenly we're kissing. Our bodies press against each other, our hungry mouths can't get enough.

When we sleep together, it is a revelation. It is intense and intoxicating. There is a moment during this first time with another woman when I clearly think to myself, 'Oh, *this* is what sex is supposed to feel like. This is how I'm supposed to feel when I have sex with someone.' And it's the first time I've ever had that thought.

Once the seal has been broken on our magnetic attraction, we have many more nights together. We tell nobody what we're doing. I'm not ready to detonate my life by coming out and neither is she. Something's starting to flicker in my mind, though. A one-off sapphic romance might have been a fluke, but now there's a reboot called Secret Sapphic 2: The Undercover Lez Strikes Back. Call me crazy, but is something going on here?

❋

It's around this time that I meet a woman who will change my life forever. Her name is Bette Porter.

So I'm back in Leeds between terms, stealth-watching *The L Word* in my teenage bedroom. *The L Word* is the most famous lesbian TV show ever made. When Ilene Chaiken's LA drama premieres in 2004, it marks a new era of representation, putting queer women front and centre.

I've locked my door, but the volume is still turned right down. I'm both terrified of being caught and extremely turned on. It's the TV equivalent of a danger-wank. I can't believe what I'm seeing. Lesbians! En masse! On the telly! Usually on the rare occasion you do spot a gay lady on TV, she is the only one, a lesbian lone wolf in a sea of straights. I've seen queer women together very occasionally in *Bad Girls* or *Tipping the Velvet*, but the characters in *The L Word* are something entirely different. They aren't from the distant past or locked up in prison for their sins. These are contemporary, free-range lesbians. I am immediately and irrevocably obsessed. I fancy them all. What is this brave new world?

Mine is not a unique experience. Queers everywhere are watching the show and feeling something they've never felt before. They feel, *we* feel, instantly less alone.

As I keep watching, my eyes are drawn to Bette Porter, played by *Flashdance* star Jennifer Beals. Bette is exquisite, always wearing an impeccably tailored trouser suit, always making a slightly inappropriate, impassioned speech. She is indifferent to men and addicted to seducing women. Part of me wants to be her and a much bigger part wants to be with her.

Also, not to state the obvious here, but *The L Word* is just *so* gay. They're always talking about exotic concepts like 'lesbian bed death' and 'big old lezzy tennis players'. I learn all the words to the iconic theme song: 'Talking, laughing, loving, breathing, fighting, fucking . . . '

Characters keep giving really specific lesbian advice and I'm taking copious mental notes: 'If you don't have bush confidence, you won't feel good about your bush and you will never get laid.' Got it, embrace your bush or no one else will.

'What do lesbians bring on a second date? A turkey baster.' I'm not much of a chef, but I dunno, I'm feeling pretty pumped right now. Maybe I can get one at Sainsbury's!

'If your ring finger is longer than your index finger, it means you're a lesbian.' Sounds bogus, but lemme quickly check. Holy shit imaginary *L Word* friends, I have Gay Finger!

The L Word is a portal to a parallel universe. It offers this sense of possibility, a blueprint for a way of being that I couldn't have fathomed before. Could this be my life? Could I be a lesbian art world mogul with a wife and a gang of cool queer pals, who goes to girl parties called Twat: The Night?

The show's impact on me doesn't end once the episode stops playing. *The L Word* acts as a gateway to a whole new community I have never experienced before, the community of fandom. I devour blogs about the show and watch YouTube supercuts of the best (AKA steamiest) scenes. I read in astonishment about viewing parties in the US and imagine being in a bar full of women who love *The L Word* as much as I do. The first ever podcast I listen to is *The Planet*, where KC and Elka, two superfans from Albuquerque, dissect each episode in minute detail. I visit fan site thelwordonline.com and am staggered by the messageboards filled with page after page of comments lusting after androgynous heartthrob Shane McCutcheon, trash-talking divisive baby gay Jenny Schecter and, most mind-blowingly of all, flirting outrageously with each other. What is making my brain explode is the fact that these comments are from actual living, lezzing people. This isn't just about characters on TV any more. These are real women-loving women in real life, bloody loads of them.

The L Word is the shared sacred text and it's suddenly giving all these far-flung queer women a common language. Online, I discover hundreds of viewers whose lives have also been transformed by the show. The internet, still a relatively recent innovation, is facilitating a whole new way for disparate LGBTQIA people to find information and each other. I don't comment on any of the messageboards. I'm not ready for that. But I know they're all there now. I know there are so many of them, all around the globe. It's as if in one instant the pitch-black night sky is lighting up with a thousand stars and they're all like me. We are legion.

While discovering *The L Word* is largely a euphoric experience, it does perhaps lead to slightly unrealistic expectations about what actual lesbian life is like. After watching the show, I go to a lesbian bar for the very first time.

Expectation: I will instantly be befriended by a posse of shimmering power dykes who will clasp me to their metaphorical, and hopefully literal, bosoms. We will bond over our shared 'bush confidence' and then probably become embroiled in a complicated yet exhilarating tangle of sexual intrigue. Sounds gay, I'm in.

Reality: After weeks of psyching myself up, getting nervous, then excited, then nervous again, I enter the bar with apprehension. I'm alone. I would never normally have come to a bar by myself, but I'm on a reconnaissance mission, and just maybe I'll meet some new amazing lesbifriends. 'All The Things She Said' by t.A.T.u. is blasting on the stereo. I feel self-conscious, out of place, even though surely this is a place where I should feel like I belong. It's not that busy, but there is a trio of women, laughing loudly. One of them looks a bit like Shane, with her messy cropped hair and studied air of being too cool to care. I'm too scared to say hello to anyone, so I order a Smirnoff Ice, scurry to the nearest corner and down the alcopop in silence. I sit. I sweat. I can't take this any more. I start pantomiming as if I've just this second remembered that I have an urgent appointment I simply must get to immediately. I beat my hasty retreat, alone, no power dyke posse in tow.

Nevertheless, *The L Word* sparks something in me and I want more of this feeling. What school didn't teach me I'm having to figure out solo, so I find myself on a quest. An undercover sapphic quest of epic proportions. My mission? To gather as much data on 'lesbians' and 'lesbianism' as possible, in an attempt to (a) understand my own sexuality, and (b) find new beauties to lust after. I'm so jazzed about this voyage of discovery! I bet I'm going to strike lesbian gold! Look out lezzies, I'm coming for you!

✻

Three weeks later.

Oh Jesus, this is bad.

Boy oh boy, it is *slim* pickings out here. Turns out there's barely any representation at all and the little there is does not exactly fill me with positive feelings about gay people. Man, this shit is bleak. According to the world of entertainment, lesbian lives are almost always steeped in tragedy and trauma. In drama, if a gay woman isn't the murderer, odds are she's the murderee. In comedy, queer women are invariably the punchline, while also being humourless fun-sponges. If you're a lesbian, you don't get to be the main character in your own life. You are a footnote in a straight person's story. You might be a butch predator or a horny femme just waiting for the right man to fix you, but you are always supporting cast. Oh, and bisexuality? Apparently no one in Hollywood has heard of it.

I watch *Chasing Amy* and *Gigli*, and discover there are not one but two films where the entire plot is 'she's a lesbian . . .

until she meets Ben Affleck', which begs the question: does Ben Affleck have an enchanted ding-dong?

Next, I settle down to watch *Basic Instinct*.

Ooh, Sharon Stone's got a girlfriend and she's called Roxy! Ding-ding-jackpot! Maybe this is a character I can relate to. Woo, go Roxy! All fancy pants, in your fancy house. I like your style, Roxy. I like your snazzy waistcoat. Yeah, you kiss Sharon Stone! Nice work, ladies!

Oh hang on . . . what the – ?

. . . What are you – ?

Roxy, stop that! No!

Roxy?!! Don't run Michael Douglas over!

STOP TRYING TO KILL PEOPLE! YOU'RE REPRESENTING THE ROXYS HERE!

. . . Oh, and now you're dead.

After Section 28's suspicious timeframe, it's starting to feel like I'm being trolled. But I am so desperate for representation, I persevere in my mission. I'm willing to sit through all manner of drivel, including some grade-A hogwash with wooden acting and dire scripts, because I've heard this rumour that two ladies graze hands and glance at each other with intent for half a second.

And then there are the films positively brimming with unrealized queer potential. Case in point: the original *A League of Their Own*, a cinematic classic set in World War Two about the first all-female pro baseball league. Love the film, love that it's all about women, and oh look, there's Madonna, this is awesome. I'm a sucker for a period drama, plus Geena Davis is a stone-cold fox. I have believed Geena Davis to be a stone-cold fox ever since that bit in *Thelma and Louise* where she's forsaken men and gone on the road with her best bud, suntanned and windswept in stonewash jeans . . . Whoops, just distracted myself for a second there. Let's get back on track. So you'd think a film about an all-female sports team would have at least one character with queer leanings, but no such luck. By the time the credits roll, I'm left with metaphorical lesbian blue balls.

❖

Thankfully, over the years that follow queer representation on-screen does start to gradually improve, with *The L Word* marking the turning point. When we watch the show back today, we can see its flaws clearly – the lack of people of colour, the casual biphobia, the horrible mishandling of the trans storyline – mistakes the show largely remedies in its 2019 reboot, *The L Word: Generation Q*. But the original show was a sea change, a landmark moment for lesbian visibility. By unapologetically centring queer female characters, it laid vital groundwork for the gay gold rush of programmes that followed, from *Lip Service* and *Sugar Rush* in the UK to *Orange Is the New Black* and *A League of Their Own* in the US.

Yes, in 2022 *A League of Their Own* is reimagined for TV and all its queer potential is finally unleashed. The reboot is replete with sapphic romances, Black queer and trans characters with agency, and even a cameo from OG cast member Rosie O'Donnell as the butch lesbian owner of a secret dyke bar. Critics rave and viewers gush. It's brilliant, it's funny, it's moving, it's joyous. And it's cancelled. Cancelled after just one season, prematurely cut short in its prime like so many other excellent queer shows from *The Wilds* to *Gentleman Jack*. Why is it that so many sapphic series face this same fate? While viewing figures and budgets play a part, I suspect misogyny and homophobia are a factor too. All too often, lesbian shows are not prioritized. They're buried in obscure time slots and seen as disposable.

That's not the only problem we're facing. The vast majority of the representation we do have is still way too white, cis and non-disabled. What we need is more, the more the better. It's not that we're greedy, it's that we've been starved. A wider landscape of content would remove the weighty burden of representing an entire community in an individual series or film. It would allow for specificity, intersectionality and compelling originality. It would make far better entertainment and make so many more people feel seen.

The reality is we don't all have identikit, cookie-cutter lives. There isn't just one queer narrative. There are infinite queer narratives, just as there are infinite narratives about straight people. So what we need is more bi stories and butch stories and trans stories. We need more nuanced, three-dimensional characters where 'lesbian' isn't the sum-total of their personality. We need queer sitcoms, queer action movies and queer prestige TV. This next bit's important: we need queer people in the positions of power, in front of and behind the camera. And we need the industry to finally understand that queer people are not a disposable commodity. We are not a fad you can roll out for ratings and then abandon when it suits you. Our stories deserve – no, scrap that. Our stories *need* to be told.

For me, there wasn't a single defining moment when a specific piece of queer representation provoked my lesbian awakening. *The L Word* was huge for me, but it wasn't as simple as seeing some characters on TV and hurtling immediately out of the closet. But every time I did see a woman kiss another woman and go unpunished, it moved the needle that little bit further towards me accepting myself. It was an incremental, cumulative effect that took years. Each frisson of recognition, every time my body involuntarily tingled in unspoken desire, those moments all mattered. Those moments gathered and grew and built on each other until there were too many to ignore.

Things I type into the Ask Jeeves search engine in 2005

What is Jet from *Gladiators* doing now?

Jet from *Gladiators* high kick

Jet from *Gladiators* hair flip

Jet from *Gladiators* sexuality?

Geena Davis sexuality?

Lucy Liu sexuality?

Lesbian films

Lesbian films where no one dies

Lesbian films by women

Why no lesbian films by women?

Lesbian illegal?

What percentage of murderers are lesbians?

How to have lesbian sex

Lesbian porn

Lesbian porn for lesbians

Why no lesbian porn for lesbians?

How do you know you're a lesbian?

How do you delete your Ask Jeeves search history?

Note: The Ask Jeeves website abruptly shut down in early 2006. To this day, I'm still not sure whether it was my randy, angst-ridden questions that did it. And the conspiracy continues . . .

CHAPTER 6

Undercover queer

Welcome to my first official date with a woman. Kiara and I have been seeing each other covertly for a while now, but on this balmy afternoon we are together and, miraculously, out of the house. To be precise, we are day-drinking al fresco in Manchester's gaybourhood. I'm nervous in case we see anyone we know, but I'm also drunk on her face, her laugh and my third glass of vodka-cranberry.

Then it happens. Kiara spots a gay guy friend of hers.

Keep calm. Stay cool. Oh god, now he's seen us. He's coming over. We've been caught lesbian-handed, being gay in Gaytown by a fellow gay. What's a closeted possible-gay to do?

'Well, well, well,' he says with a knowing smile.

Oh shit, we've been rumbled.

'Look at you straights, clogging up Canal Street!'

Say what now?

We do not correct him. We do not tell him we are actually a couple. We do not say we are queer. Instead, we chuckle along like mad straight women, half at the absurd irony of our predicament, half out of pure relief.

❋

The first time I come out in any real sense of the word, it's to a total stranger who I am 99.9 per cent sure I will never see again. The stakes couldn't be lower. Merely testing the homosexual waters, I am sending the gay canary down the mine to see if it survives. On a night out, I'm stood at the bar waiting ages to be served. The woman next to me strikes up a conversation out of extreme boredom and mild inebriation. She says her boyfriend will be annoyed the drinks are taking so long. I casually mention – easy, breezy, no big deal – that I have a girlfriend. I have not said these words out loud before. I try to sound relaxed and nonchalant, while mentally bracing myself for her reaction. I search her face for her response. She snorts with laughter, 'No, you don't.'

And there it is. The categorical denial of the possibility of my queerness. A stranger assuming she knows me better than I know myself. She either thinks I'm taking the mick, lying to make myself seem more interesting, or that I am that rare creature, a twenty-one-year-old with an imaginary friend.

I try again, 'No really, I have a girlfriend. We've been together for a few months.' Bar girl remains unconvinced.

'Yeah, right,' she replies, the sarcasm in her voice practically dripping all over the counter. She starts to edge away and I am left totally discombobulated. I've been hiding my girl-friends for years now and then when I finally muster up the courage to tell someone about one, that person flatly refuses to believe she exists.

It's your classic case of femme invisibility, something I

don't yet have the vocabulary for but will become a recurring motif of my life. Femme invisibility is the infuriating yet commonplace phenomenon of people assuming that you must be straight because you have long hair and wear lipstick. There is an oddly farcical energy to its ludicrous merry-go-round cycle: me trying desperately to hide my queerness, then finally plucking up the courage to reveal it, only to have people literally laugh in my face because the notion of me being gay is so preposterous, so I then have to really double down and try extra hard to convince them of the very thing I was previously trying so desperately to conceal.

What was the point of all those years of being so painstakingly discreet? Why did I trouble myself with so much subterfuge? The rigmarole of secret trysts and manufacturing 'crushes' on Peter Andre. I needn't have bothered. My skirt provided all the camouflage I needed. Ah, the land of missed opportunities. I could have been slap-bang at the front of every Pride parade, brandishing a humungous banner reading, 'Massive lesbian right here!' and onlookers would have assumed I was holding it for a pal.

To many, the facts of who I am are unfathomable. In their eyes, feminine appearance does not a lesbian make. This is femmephobia in action and femmephobia is a feminist issue. So is butchphobia. Both prejudices stem from limiting ideas of what a woman 'should' be. Society judges us on what we look like and proceeds to make sweeping generalizations cobbled together through lazy stereotypes, false assumptions and a heavy dose of misogyny. By default, women are still defined in relation to men, so when many people see a feminine woman, they assume a man must somehow be involved. They do not pause to consider that she – *that I* – might be gay. Is it really so big a mental leap to think that a girl who likes girly stuff might also like girls?

Kiara and I are both in possession of flowing locks and overflowing make-up bags. Therefore, in public we are read as two straight women, even if we're holding hands and staring into each other's eyes adoringly. This doesn't just happen in predominantly straight spaces. On multiple occasions we try to go to gay bars, only to be interrogated because the bouncers don't believe we're a couple. It's like we are having to audition to play the roles of the queer women we actually are. The casting director/security guard doesn't want to give us the part because we just don't have 'the right look'. So we are forced to try and prove our validity as queer people to access our safe spaces, despite the fact that we are literally the target clientele. I lose count of the number of times I am denied entry to a gay club because I 'don't look like a lesbian'. I'm not sure how to improve my chances. Should I be accessorizing my ensemble with a rainbow stripy strap-on?

❋

I'm starting to fall hard for Kiara. In fact, my feelings are running so high I'm acting a bit too eager, embarrassingly overkeen. I can feel myself doing it, but I don't know how to not do it. One day in my room, I'm gazing at her like a lovesick puppy who's recently discovered the life-changing magic of lesbian shagging. I'm not playing it cool. I'm a bundle of excited, horny, sappy feelings and I'm showing them all to her without restraint. I tell her how into what we're doing I am, how into *her* I am.

She looks me dead in the eyes and says, ever so coolly but with crushing certainty, 'You and me – you do know this isn't anything serious?'

I am devastated. More than that, I am humiliated. I have exposed my authentic emotional self and had a metaphorical pie to the face. How could I have let myself get so carried away and not realized she was just here for sex and giggles?

Silly Rox. Always too much. Always making a fool of myself.

And so, I take her at her word. I think, *Alright then, if this is just sex and giggles, then sure, I can do sex and giggles.* I do not end things. I want the sex and giggles.

We carry on our liaisons, but from that moment I hold a part of myself back. The pure, enthusiastic, unbridled part. She does not want that. But something peculiar happens. The emotions I spilled out to her at the start, she begins to express those same feelings for me. She gazes at me with a new intensity. She talks about love and a future where we are together. She tells me, 'I like everything about you – your personality, your sense of humour, your looks. If I found all that in a guy, I'd be married by now.' I wonder how differently things might have played out if she hadn't told me to calm down my tidal wave of feelings so early on. Perhaps we could have had something extraordinary.

But I have held all my falling-in-love feelings back for so long, when I reach for them now I find they are no longer there. I start to feel anxious when we are together. I realize we are not on the same page. I need to end this before it gets any more out of hand.

❊

When it doesn't work out with Kiara, I go on dates with men that I know in my heart won't lead anywhere. In my teens and twenties, I try so hard to be straight. When that strategy fails pitifully, I try even harder to be bi.

I want to be very clear here: bisexuality is real and valid. In the 2021 UK Census, 1.3 per cent of people over the age of sixteen identify as bisexual. There is widespread biphobia, both insidious and overt. But to some of the people in my life, it feels like telling them I'm bisexual might be an easier pill for them to swallow, probably due to the biphobic myth that bi women always end up with men anyway. So I try. I try in vain. I keep that door slightly ajar, giving guys 'one last go', just to make absolutely sure.

My dates with men are very different to the ones with Kiara. They feel more like hanging out with mates, but with an added element of me conducting field research. I am never fully present on these dates, because I am always partly in my own head trying to decipher exactly how I feel about being with a guy.

As for the men, there's the aspiring musician who tells me he loves me on our first date. I'm flattered, but unable to reciprocate. There's the barman with the beautiful face, who I think would make a stunning drag queen. And then there's the tall, handsome man who I realize midway through the evening is almost definitely a fellow closeted homosexual. Let's call him Elton.

Elton takes me to an arthouse cinema showing a black and white documentary with subtitles about something very serious and political. To be honest, I'm not really paying attention, not because I'm overcome with lust but because something is off and I can't put my finger on it.

Ten minutes in, he leans towards me and whispers in my ear. It is not a sweet nothing or a flirty remark. It is instead his opinion on the clothes the very serious political people on-screen are wearing. This jarring sartorial commentary isn't cast-iron proof that Elton's gay by any means. Neither is the fact that he's exceptionally well groomed. Nor the way that, during our post-film beverage, he keeps steering the conversation back to one of the men in the film and talking about how he was so 'amazing' and 'ripped'. But my spidey senses are tingling. My gaydar is twitching.

Here we are, roleplaying a heterosexual date, only it's not very convincing. It's like we're doing an awkward impersonation of straight people. I wonder if we're both silently wishing we were on a date with someone of the same gender. So, what are we doing here? Who are we doing this for? My best guess: our parents.

Elton is very good-looking and very charming. He smells great too and genuinely does have some fascinating insights about fashion, yet I really, really don't want to kiss him. So much so that at the end of the night, I blurt out a manic 'Bye then!' and leg it in the wrong direction, looking fully unhinged but not caring because I'm so desperate to avoid a possible goodnight snog between two possible closeted gays.

This might seem like bizarre behaviour, but coming out, even just to yourself, is no easy thing. In my case it's not as straightforward as: I have a couple of secret girlfriends, see a few lesbians on TV, then proudly claim my identity with no hesitation. It's tempting to cling to that reassuringly neat little narrative, but the truth is so much more fraught, non-linear and human than that. There's a lifetime of unlearning to do, an awful lot of emotional baggage to unpack and countless last-ditch attempts to just be 'normal'. As women we're conditioned to make ourselves palatable. It would be tragic to say that I pretend to fancy men for almost a decade to try and make people like me. But you know, it's not *not* true.

It's such a disconcerting, knotty thing to unravel, this internal tangle of how others see me vs how I feel inside, my desire to be a 'good', 'acceptable' woman vs my desire to do 'bad', 'unacceptable' things with other women. Throw wobbly self-esteem in the mix and hey presto, the perfect recipe for a closeted lez.

So no, me fully realizing I'm not straight or bi is not straight-forward. It's convoluted, protracted, a saga not a scene. There is an in-depth process of risk assessment, mental recalibration and a great re-imagining of what my life might look like. Inevitably I catastrophize. I fret about how it will make other people feel, how I will feel saying it out loud, the abuse I might face, the otherness, the second-class citizen-ness, the fear of what will happen if I go down this path, the fear of what will happen if I don't. As I hold my soul up to the spotlight on long, dark nights, the key question I ask myself is this: how much would I be prepared to sacrifice to live this life? Also: who would I be if nobody else could see or judge? I smugly reckon I would still be quite a nice person. I am grimly certain I would be gay.

There's another factor at play here too. The word 'lesbian' worries me. Growing up, I never hear the word 'lesbian' used in a positive light. 'Lesbian' is the butt of the joke. It is always pronounced with venom, disgust or mocking, put-you-in-your-place laughter. 'Lesbian' is an attack word in the arsenal of the playground bully. A missile fired on a mission to hurt and humiliate. 'Lesbian' is a target on your back, because 'lesbian' is shorthand for: 'You don't fit in. You have failed at femininity. You are the modern-day equivalent of a witch and we are on a witch-hunt.' 'Lesbian' is the word for a woman who is womaning wrong. Now I am no fan of the patriarchy, but even I have to admit this is a very clever trick they've played. To weaponize this particular word. To make this the thing a woman desperately does not want to be called. Because what is a lesbian, after all? A woman who neither needs nor wants a man. And what could be a bigger threat to the patriarchal world order than that?

So, as I'm grappling with the whole 'Am I? Aren't I?' dilemma, this word is bothering me. Declaring myself to be 'a lesbian' feels like a big, scary thing because it is a big, scary word. I really wish it didn't sound so serious and scientific. It's almost clinical, like a specimen in a lab, or a rare breed of alien lifeform. And I wish 'lesbian' didn't have quite so many syllables. It takes so much more time to pronounce than a laidback 'gay' or 'bi'. It is a word that is easy to trip up on, especially if the word itself makes you nervous. So I resist the word 'lesbian'. It is the word I do not want to say.

There is another word that has burrowed its way into my marrow. A word I try not to think about, because it provokes such a visceral reaction in me. The word is freak. Freak is how I feel. At the time, I feel so much shame. In later years that shame will be replaced with anger, not towards myself but towards the society that conditioned me to feel so horrendous about my identity, to fear and loathe the word 'lesbian', the very word that describes what I am. We should not be made to hide and hate ourselves. In the future I will become that angry lesbian I was terrified of being perceived as, but it won't feel shameful. It will feel powerful.

✻

Flash forward to the present day and my feelings about this word have changed dramatically. This is due in part to the fact that I now use it on a daily basis in my job. 'Lesbian' is a tool of my trade. I have been exposed to 'lesbian' so many times that 'lesbian' doesn't frighten me any more. I wield the word 'lesbian' with ease and authority, although I note that the word still makes those around me nervous.

I secretly enjoy that it holds the power to shock a room. It has heat. It is transgressive. I used to find it cumbersome and embarrassing; now I find it muscular and mighty. I relish its heft. Sometimes I like to make it even longer by adding a swashbuckling adjective in front of it, like 'dedicated' or 'rampant'. Giving a speech at an LGBTQIA film festival I recently announced with gusto, 'I am a raging lesbian.' The audience laughed and cheered and it felt immense. There is power in reclaiming the word 'lesbian', embracing it, owning it, and uttering it without self-consciousness or hesitation.

But the word still makes me angry, not because of lesbians themselves. I am a big fan of them as a genre. But because of the way that I, and other lesbians, have been conditioned to hate this term that describes us. I worry that young lesbians don't want to be associated with it, for all the same reasons I resisted it for so long, but for troubling new ones too. A 2022 study by LGBTQIA youth charity Just Like Us shows that two-thirds of young lesbians in the UK delay coming out due to harmful stereotypes: 'being cringey or awkward', 'wrong', 'masculine or butch', 'over-sexualized', 'unattractive', 'man-hating', 'old-fashioned' and, alarmingly, 'anti-trans'.

What I want to say to these young lesbians who hesitate to come out for these reasons is this:

Oh, my darling. I have been where you are and let me tell you, people who scorn lesbians are fuckwits. Do not let fuck-wits control your life.

You can be any kind of lesbian you want to be. You can be butch, femme, trans, non-binary or cis.

Being a lesbian is not old-fashioned. It is Vintage. It is Classic. Because we have always been here and we always will be.

Being a lesbian does not mean you are wrong or unattract-ive or anti-trans. You are who you are and that is absolutely right. You can be beautiful, you can be handsome, you can be a trans ally, and still be a lesbian. None of these things are mutually exclusive. It is a revolutionary act to come out as a lesbian when you defy the stereotypes. In coming out, you prove all those fuckers wrong. You shift misconceptions.

Do not let other people define you. It is good and it is glorious to be a lesbian. Lesbians of the past, your queer ancestors, fought for you to be able to own this word. So go ahead and claim it to honour them and honour yourself.

Enjoy it. Bloody relish it. Say it out loud, even if it is just in the privacy of your own bedroom. Say it until saying it doesn't make you flinch. Say it with pride and self-love. Say it with verve and panache and fire in your eyes. Savour every last one of its many syllables.

You can be a lesbian, my darling. You can be whatever you are.

Things I have said to bouncers at gay clubs

'Yes, I do know this is a gay bar because I am, in fact, gay.'

'No really, I'm very, very gay.'

'What do you mean I don't look like a lesbian? I am a lesbian and this is what I look like.'

'Can we not? I just want to party with my people.'

'I'm a lesbian. Seriously. I'll prove it. I can name, like, all the characters in *The L Word*. Shane! Bette! Dana! Dana's cat, Mr Pickles! What more do you want from me?!'

'Look, I should warn you. I know literally all the lyrics to *The L Word* theme tune and if you don't let me in, I will have no choice but to sing them at you until you can't take it any more.'

'Sandi Toksvig is my auntie!' (She's not.) 'You wait till she hears about this!'

'Please stop oppressing me. I just want to drink cheap wine and dance with my brethren to Kylie's cheesiest hits.'

'Femme lesbians are real and valid and deserve to get embarrassingly smashed with their friends.'

'I'm a lesbian. I read *DIVA* magazine.'

'I'm a lesbian. I write for *DIVA* magazine.'

'I'm a lesbian. I am the editor-in-chief of *DIVA* magazine. Don't believe me? Hang on . . . This is my photo on the

DIVA website. Now please let me in or I *will* write an article about this.'

'You do know you're literally stopping gay patrons from entering this gay bar . . . Oh my god. Are you the real reason gay nightlife is dying out?'

'Yes, I really am gay. Why else would a woman *this* glamorous have nails *this* short?'

CHAPTER 7

The truth about coming out

I wish I could say that the first time I fall in proper, full-blown, grown-up love with another woman begins in a super dreamy, super gay meet-cute scenario, that we play on the same football team or, in the women's section of an independent bookshop we both reach for the same copy of *The Feminine Mystique*. The setting for our first encounter is prosaic and not particularly queer, but it is where our grand romance begins.

✤

I graduate into a recession and job prospects are bleak, especially if you want to do something as frivolous and impossible as being creative for a living. Strapped for cash, I move back to my mum's place in Leeds. After my liberating adventures in Manchester, it is deeply dispiriting to be in the confines of my old room once more. This feels like a step backwards, a reluctant return to the scene of so much unhappiness. There is a disconnect between who I was the last time I lived here, a celibate sixth former, and who I am now, a twenty-something woman who has tasted a little of life and is eager for more. I don't talk to my mum about the more scandalous details of what I've been up to. I keep those parts hidden and resign myself to this smaller, more dismal existence. I am once again in my teenage bedroom with its lilac walls, navy carpet and the patterned curtains I didn't choose.

I look into applying for an MA in Journalism, but the hefty fees are beyond my means. I audition for drama school, get a place but can't afford the tuition. I am unsuccessful in my attempts to secure a job as an editorial assistant or a copy-writer or anything remotely connected to something I might actually want to do. Needs must when times are tough, so I take a job at a call centre selling insurance.

Every day I catch the bus into town, trudge through a revolving door into a concrete building and speak to people who don't want to speak to me, trying to persuade them to do something they don't want to do, and quite frankly I don't think they should.

I work in a vast open-plan office decorated in shades of greige. It's not your typical romantic setting for a life-changing romance to blossom, but it is where I first see Robyn. Our eyes meet across a crowded call centre. I am instantly intrigued. She is unlike any woman I've ever seen before, with her cropped hair, strong jawline and twinkly eyes. She's also got this particular energy about her, a no-nonsense, purposeful vigour. When she cruises past my desk with her jacket collar turned up, I experience a bolt of lust. The first time I see her I know two things in my bones: 1. she is gay and 2. I really fancy her.

From past experience, I'm aware she may not read me as queer. So I overcompensate by making deliberate, lingering eye contact with her. I'm trying to get the right balance of signalling I'm interested without being offputtingly intense. I'm not sure it's working. But then I hear that she's been asking about me.

On the next work night out, I might have the chance to discover whether she fancies me too. I'm getting ready for the evening ahead. Knowing she'll be there, I have planned my ensemble with precision, agonized over my hairdo, reapplied my winged eyeliner three times, workshopped my entire wardrobe and ended up wearing the first thing I tried on anyway. All this time, I'm playing 'Tonight' from *West Side Story* on my CD player on repeat and singing along with gusto. 'Tonight, tonight, won't be just any night,' I croon. Wow, perhaps I'm not straight or a lesbian – maybe I'm a gay man after all!

What I have not prepared for is the downpour. How did I spend so long strategizing my outfit and still neglect to pack an umbrella? In romcoms when the leading lady gets caught in the rain, she somehow becomes even more beautiful, her eyes bright, her skin glistening. But the movie industry lied to me. Forget dewy angel, I'm more drowned rat.

By the time I arrive at the club, my hair, the same hair I spent forty-five minutes styling, is literally dripping. Panic-stricken and sopping wet, I make a beeline for the ladies and desperately try to repair the extensive weather-damage. I dab frantically at my blurry make-up with scraps of bog roll. I dry my entire body, outfit and hair, two inches at a time, under the tiny blast of hot air from the hand-dryer. I do my best to look presentable but it's a bodge-job. I can't give up now though, because Robyn has arrived.

We end up talking for hours, splitting off from the group and sequestering in our own corner of the seating area. She has a broad Yorkshire accent and she is funny, very funny. We laugh and we flirt and we drink each other in with our eyes. At some point in the night, I realize that without saying a word about it, our fingers have found each other and we are now holding hands. We leave the club, but we don't want to leave each other.

In the early hours of the morning, we walk around the centre of Leeds, the rain-sodden pavement glinting in the moonlight. Our first kiss happens opposite McDonald's. I have never kissed another woman in the open air. It has always been indoors in locked rooms. There's no way I'd risk this in the daytime, yet here I am under the romantic glow of Maccy D's Golden Arches. I am kissing a woman with short hair in the centre of the city I grew up in. In the immortal words of Ronald, 'I'm lovin' it!'

✻

In typical sapphic fashion, our romance is fast-tracked and full on. Staying up all night because we can't get enough of each other becomes a regular occurrence. We talk endlessly, fascinated by the minutiae of one another. We binge-watch *The L Word* before binge-watching is a thing. She introduces me to actually enjoyable lesbian films like *Bound* and *Imagine Me & You*, except we never manage to get to the end of one. We're always snogging each other's faces off within the first fifteen minutes.

In the beginning, when it is just us two, it is a perfect bubble. One day we are in the kitchen in her terraced sharehouse. I am dressed in her pyjamas, sitting on the worktop. She stands in front of me and I wrap my legs around her. My arms are draped around her neck. I kiss her and I hold her face in my hands and I have never felt like this before. I know without a doubt that I am in love with this woman. In a matter of weeks, she has become my entire world. But in this moment, despite all the lust and the love, there is fear too. I'm scared by the strength of my emotions, scared about how much this will blow my life up and petrified of how my family will react.

I have also already noticed that Robyn is a dominant character. She is plain-speaking and opinionated, much more so than me. I like this about her. I find her confidence sexy. It makes the tender, intimate moments feel even more miraculous, as if I am the only person in the world who gets to see this soft side of her. I can already feel my overwhelming desire to please her. On a recent night out, I saw a flash of alcohol-infused jealousy in her eyes. She accused me of flirting with someone I absolutely wasn't flirting with. I reassured her and consciously dialled down my natural friendliness to keep her calm. This troubles me. But I can't resist the pull between us. I know that I am hopelessly in love with her and I must ride this love wherever it takes me.

Back to that old joke that goes, 'What does a lesbian bring on a second date?' It's such a well-worn gag it has not one but three possible punchlines: she brings a turkey baster / moving van / marriage licence. Now I know I said all that stuff before about bogus stereotypes, but I have to concede that this one may have some truth in it, at least that's been my experience.

Perhaps we often move so fast because we women can be so in tune with our feelings. We can empathize with each other and connect over our shared experiences. It is also true that our relationships exist outside the mainstream, so maybe we don't feel so much pressure to follow rigid dating rules or play hard to get. Put two of us who have a lot of feelings about each other together and behold, uncharted realms of emotional intimacy. Everything is magnified. Lust! Friendship! Deep And Meaningfuls! Giggle fits! Tenderness! Trauma bonding! Passion! I can't speak to how it feels to be a besotted heterosexual, but I can confirm that this lady love stuff is flipping phenomenal.

Our first few months together are heady and gorgeous, but they are also eye-opening. When we are out in public, people react differently to how they did with me and Kiara. With her short hair and bare face, Robyn is read as a lesbian, so I am now part of a visibly queer couple. If we walk hand in hand through the streets, we are often met with confusion, anger and sometimes vile homophobic abuse. There's this sense

I get from some men that they feel Robyn has stolen a woman that is their rightful property. And that really pisses them off.

Unless we're in a straight bar. In that environment, it piques a man's interest. This is just like his favourite film and his favourite film is a porno. You can practically see the ticker tape scrolling through his head: 'Ding, ding, threesome.' What he says out loud: 'Can I join in?' Or the closely related and equally seedy, 'Can I watch?'

I meet so many creeps whose eyes light up like a slot machine as soon as they twig that my gal pal is actually my other half. Oh, did I say other half? Sorry, obviously I meant other third because until a bloke comes swaggering into our lives, we're incomplete. Although some men might fantasize about a three-way with a lesbian couple, here's what that would look like in real life: the man feeling indescribably awkward while I lecture him on intersectional feminism – fully clothed – and my girlfriend contemplates whacking him in the crotch with a spanner. We're gay: we've got tools!

Why do some men do this? Why do they have to place themselves in the centre of something that clearly has bupkis to do with them? Why this need to insert themselves into our same-sex sexuality? They seem stumped by an age-old question: why do lesbians lesbian? Which man are we trying to impress with our otherwise inexplicable lesbian behaviour? It's like they just cannot get their heads around the idea that women could want to be with each other, no man involved. If a lesbian falls in the forest and a man's not there to catch her, is she still a lesbian? The correct answer is, of course, Hell, yes. A lesbian with bruised knees maybe, but a sapphic all the same.

Maybe it's about the lure of the unattainable, or the disproportionately high volume of lesbian porn, but I think there's another factor at play here: male entitlement to female bodies. Certain men assume that they are what's missing in the bedroom of a female couple. This is blatant sexism. It's linked to how those same men too often view women's bodies as open season for commentary, unsolicited touching or worse. To get technical, it's a case of misogyny multiplied by homophobia, because our relationships are seen as inherently less-than. But these men have missed the fundamental point of lesbianism. It's not about turning guys on; it's about turning girls on.

Homophobic abuse and unwanted propositions for gang bangs aside, things are going well with Robyn. She tells me that she has a plane ticket to Australia, leaving in a matter of months. Would I ever consider going with her? Of course, I bloody would.

So it is, in the end, love, the unstoppable, dizzying, euphoric, slightly unhinged force of first true love, that finally propels me out of the closet to my family. To be completely honest, if I had never fallen this hard for a woman, I may well never have come out to them. I was too scared of how they would react. Their approval means too much to me. It always has. I so badly want them to be proud of me and I know, deep down, they are unlikely to be proud of this. But ultimately, there is a force in me that is now stronger than the fear I have nursed for all these years. It is for my love of her that I am finally willing to take this monumental risk, to share this thing about myself I have always kept hidden from them until now. Also, I have to explain why I'm suddenly off to Oz.

❋

Let's talk about coming out for a minute. Should we even have to come out? It's not like heterosexuals have to come out. Why should the onus be on the queer person to correct straight people about their incorrect, and frankly lazy, heteronormative assumptions?

As queer folks know, coming out isn't a one-time thing.

There can be people you're out to and people you aren't. I don't fully come out to everyone in my life until I start writing about being gay for a living, at which point the jig is well and truly up. My CV now outs me.

Coming out is a thing you have to do over and over again and the truth is, I don't always do it. I come out on a case-by-case basis. My antennae perk up, hyper-aware of myriad factors so I can make a split-second judgement call. It's like *Mission Impossible* laser beams are suddenly criss-crossing all over the place. I'm making mental calculations at lightning speed, asking myself quickfire questions. Do I feel safe? Are there any signs they might be homophobic or misogynistic? How tough am I feeling today? Could I handle a negative reaction? Can I even be arsed to deal with intrusive questions or unwelcome opinions?

*

Before I come out to my parents, I have to come out to the others in my life, so I set off on The Coming Out Tour, which is not nearly as rock and roll as it sounds. It happens in stages. First, I perform a sapphic rite of passage, take the plunge and two antihistamines, and come out to my cat. Whisky, bless his paws, is really sweet about it. As I softly weep into his fur, he purrs away reassuringly and then snuggles up closer. He still loves me. This has changed nothing between us, except that one of us is going to be getting extra meaty moggy biscuits later.

I come out to my friends next. I'm pretty nervous about this one, so Whisky and I rehearse the conversations extensively, preparing for all possible outcomes. Then I psych myself up to tell them, taking deep breaths to retain my composure. How will they take my big gay news? What will they say about this staggering personal revelation?

To be honest, it's all a bit of an anti-climax. My furry friend was way more surprised than this lot. My mates are, for the most part, totally lovely and unfazed about it, which makes sense. After all, they did stick by me when I was shouting about my vag all over town. A few tell me they've known for a while, to which I reply, 'Well, why the dickens didn't you tell me?!'

Then there's my parents. I come out to my father over what I can confidently describe as the least enjoyable Bella Italia meal of either of our lives. Sweating profusely, I pluck up the courage to say the thing. I tell him I'm going to Australia with my partner and my partner is a woman. I gabble, 'I just thought you should know. We can speak about it . . . or not . . . '

Then follows the most painfully awkward silence in the history of painfully awkward silences. Eventually he speaks. To his credit, he manages a joke: 'Changing the subject now would be as if there was a giant pink elephant in the room and I was peeping around it to say, "How's the weather?"' We laugh disproportionately loudly at this, a subconscious attempt to defuse the overwhelming tension filling the air.

We then go on to discuss . . . climate change, carbonara, anything else we can come up with so that we don't have to talk about the giant pink lesbian elephant standing in the middle of this chain restaurant, waving her ostentatiously homosexual trunk at us wildly. We maintain this strategy for the next forty-five minutes. And sixteen years.

We rarely talk about The Lesbian Stuff again and he never meets any of my girlfriends. To be fair, if I wanted to introduce him to my partner I'm pretty sure he would show up and be polite, but in all honesty I don't want to put any of us through the ordeal. I'm still traumatized by that wretched lunch. I haven't been able to look at a spag bol the same way since.

When I come out to my mum she replies flippantly, 'That's fine. As long as you marry a man and have children first.' I'm not entirely sure if she's joking. I wait for her to laugh. No laugh comes. She tells me, 'You don't look like a lesbian.'

Over time I understand that my mum would prefer me to be straight and in a relationship with a man. She has some outlandish suggestions for who these men should be, regularly bringing up the names of actual Hollywood A-listers as potential suitors. I calmly advise her that even if I was straight, I don't think it's realistic to expect Brad Pitt for a son-in-law. And yes, Affleck's name is mentioned too. Well done, Ben. You've done it again.

After my disastrous coming out to my parents, I do not want to come out to my granny. She is too precious to me to risk damaging our relationship. I'm worried that being from an older generation might make it harder for her to understand. And I cannot bear the thought of our connection, the connection that has always been my safest, happiest place, being tarnished.

But the decision is taken out of my hands because my mum decides to out me to her. When I find this out, my heart drops into my stomach. I need to talk to her, need to try and explain. This is urgent. So I visit her. We sit together in her living room, as we have done many times before, but it feels different. I never feel awkward with her, but today I do.

Nervously, I broach the subject. 'Mum said she spoke to you . . . about me and Robyn.'

'Ye-e-e-s,' she says carefully.

We talk for a long time. She tells me she is worried that being a lesbian isn't safe. She has seen all those newspaper headlines about lesbian serial killers. I tell her that is tabloid sensationalism and the vast majority of lesbians haven't murdered anyone at all. She accepts that. But then she tells me she is even more worried that if this is my life, I won't ever be able to find a happy, fulfilling relationship like the one she had with my grandad. I tell her that my *only* chance of finding a romance half that wonderful is to be with a woman. She nods slowly, tenderly, taking this in. As I talk, she listens. Really listens. I tell her I'm terrified that me being with a woman will change how she feels about me. She tells me she loves me and she always will.

Out of all my family, my granny is by the far the kindest about me being gay. When I take Robyn to meet her, my granny is warm and welcoming. Afterwards she tells me how much she likes Robyn and says she is glad to see me happy.

My mum, on the other hand, is not so enthusiastic about my new partner. One day Robyn drives me to my mum's so I can grab a few of my things. I give her strict instructions to stay put in the car. I assure her I'll only be a minute and then we can scuttle back to the safety of her place. There is no world in which I want her and my mum to meet. I know that would end in disaster.

I head inside and greet my mum with false positivity. I'm striving for upbeat and breezy. No big deal. Nothing to see here. Everybody, be cool! I go upstairs and start grabbing what I need in a hurry. A couple of books, my perfume, favourite photos of me with Lela and me with my granny. Then I hear something that stops me in my tracks. Voices. Two women's voices.

Shitshitshitshit.

This can't be happening. I hurtle down the stairs two at a time and burst through the living room door. My mum is there. And so is Robyn. My two worlds are colliding. It is a train crash that I cannot stop happening. It is too late. This cannot be undone.

Neither of them has been comfortable enough to take a seat or polite enough to offer one, so they are standing, two metres apart, staring daggers at each other. I do not know what has been said, but the mood is far from friendly. It's not even a slightly awkward small-talk-type situation either. They look like two primates in a standoff, rival alphas asserting their dominance and I am the territory they are battling over. I make a limp, desperate quip, 'Ah, so I take it you've met.'

I will later learn that while I was upstairs my mum went out to Robyn's car, opened the door and insisted she come inside. Right now, I just know that the thing I really didn't want to happen is happening and it feels more hostile than I could have anticipated in my worst catastrophizing nightmare. I babble a lame excuse, as if I've just remembered we're late for a thing. I promise my mum I'll call her soon and we beat a hasty retreat.

But from that short encounter it is clear to me that Robyn and my mum do not like each other. They aren't just uncomfortable because they are strangers. It's much deeper and more primal than that. There is distrust and unease and defensiveness and protectiveness going both ways. Robyn thinks my mum's behaviour was odd, that her manner was abrupt, that she was judging her. She is correct on all counts. My mum takes an instant dislike to Robyn too.

This is not a case of a dodgy first meeting that eventually smooths over into a friendly or even tolerably polite relationship. Their instant distrust turns quickly into bald contempt on both sides. Once again, I am caught in the crossfire of two people I love who can't stand each other. If I had a time machine I would go back and never let Robyn venture within a mile radius of my mum's place. I would have caught the bloody bus. I do not want my mum to know my girlfriend. It is better for all three of us if she doesn't.

I don't blame Robyn for disliking someone who makes no attempt to hide her disdain for her. I also understand that my mum is finding this new situation difficult. But I wish they could both put my feelings first. I wish they could at least try and make some sort of effort for the sake of me, the one thing they have in common, the person they both say they love so fiercely.

Since that meeting I have been at home even less. I can't bear to wade through the bristly atmosphere to make clunky small talk or confronting big talk. I don't want to talk about any of it with my mum. I don't want to argue. I don't want to open up. I want what seems like the only option at this point: a double life.

There's a popular coming-out narrative that declares motivationally, 'it gets better'. 'My parents didn't like me being gay at first, but in time they came round and now they adore my partner' – that kind of thing. At first, I cling onto these 'it gets better' stories, but in time I start to resent them. They do not reflect my experience.

With support from Robyn and Lela, I process what has happened and make a decision. I will not keep putting myself in the position of trying to convince them to be ok with this. It is too corrosive for me to stay in that place. It is eating away at something essential in me. How can I get over my own internalized shame about being gay when the people I love are mirroring it right back at me? After giving it a few years, and then a few years more, I am utterly exhausted by it all. For my own good and the good of my relationships with them, eventually I give up. I finally learn to accept their lack of acceptance. Ultimately, it is about preservation. I want to preserve my relationships with them, but I also need to preserve my relationship with myself.

This hurts. Of course it does. But the false hope hurts more. So I deliberately swerve potentially fraught conversation topics. As I really do live a very gay existence, that means a lot of aspects of my life are out of bounds: my relationships, my community, my career. I wonder if part of the reason I end up gravitating towards the work I do is about seeking the relief of existing in a world where queerness is celebrated. And I don't want other queer people to feel unworthy or alone. I understand how painful that can be. But I make my peace with the reality of how it is and let go of the fantasy of how I wish it was. That's enough of that now.

What I've learned is this. Family reactions to a queer person coming out aren't a simple dichotomy. Option a: tearful revelation followed by trauma and tragedy. Option b: nervous announcement greeted with enthusiasm and lots of cuddles. As with so many things in life, binary thinking does not begin to reflect the reality of our lived experiences. There is a grey area in this gay area. But a grey area is not the end of the world. It's a situation you can figure out how to navigate. Your parents don't need to be the ones you get that all-embracing love of every fibre of your being from. You can find that from friends, partners or community, and when you do it is liberating and so deeply healing.

My coming out story is not a sob story. It's a story of acceptance, but it's not so much about securing acceptance from other people. It's more about me accepting that this is who I am and I cannot change how others feel and both of those things are ok. There is life and love and queer joy to be found beyond all of that.

Although I must admit, every time I'm at a Pride parade and the Parents and Friends Of Lesbians and Gays group marches past, when I spot the beaming middle-aged woman wearing a T-shirt with the slogan 'I love my gay son', there's a sudden unbidden swell of emotion in my chest. I am so happy for this mum and her child, but I also find it almost unbearably moving. There's a pang. But then that pang dissipates, and I keep marching.

The coming out kit of dreams

I've often thought it would be great if when you came out you were instantly presented with a readymade coming out kit. You'd speak your truth, then someone wise, awesome and twinkly like Lily Tomlin or Dolly Parton would suddenly materialize in a cloud of rainbow glitter. So basically it works like the tooth fairy, but super turbo gay. Your fairy gaymother would give you a reassuring 'welcome to the club' hug and produce a perfectly curated, personalized coming out kit from her handbag.

Here's what I'd have in mine:

The gift of flawless gaydar

A can of homophobe repellent to ward off the pests

The L Word box set, all seasons

A feelgood playlist including 'This Is Me' from *The Greatest Showman*, 'I'm Coming Out' by Diana Ross and 'Beautiful' by Christina Aguilera

One rainbow stripy prom dress, sparkly

One rainbow stripy cake with icing saying 'Congratugaytions!'

One copy of *The Lesbian Kama Sutra* (it's a real book!)

Lesbian ID card granting instant access to gay bars, no interrogation needed

Bag of confetti to celebrate if it went well

Box of Kleenex in case it didn't

CHAPTER 8

Get the party started

I'm on a gay pub crawl in Leeds in a state of wide-eyed wonderment. I can't wrap my head around my hometown having enough queer venues to facilitate these shenanigans. To think, I spent so much of my adolescence alone in my room feeling isolated, when just a twenty-minute bus ride away lay a veritable cornucopia of delights. This whole thriving community was right there on my doorstep. I was oblivious to the fact that Leeds was a hotbed of homosexuality all along.

Robyn and I bounce from gay watering hole to gay watering hole. We stop by Blayds for a quick drink. At Viaduct Showbar we watch drag queens in sequin gowns rib the audience and pray they don't pick on us next. Finally, we end up at The New Penny. It's been going since 1953, making it one of the oldest gay bars not only in Leeds, but in the whole country – a fact that is commemorated in 2016 with a historical blue plaque. Right now, I know it as the place everyone falls into when the other bars shut. It's where we go when we don't want our night to end – loud, crowded, messy and so much fun.

Tonight, Leeds' gay scene is my safe haven. Yes, it's just getting tipsy in bars to a soundtrack of cheesy pop, but it is also, in its own sloppy-drunk way, beautiful, liberating and almost profound. After all that hiding away, all that being queer and tortured on my tod, all the pain of coming out to my family, I am not only out of the closet but out of the house and among my people. I feel the tension ease out of my shoulders. I relax into my queerness and get another round in.

There is one thing I notice though. The bars are nearly all filled with men. Are the rumours true that queer women only ever go out to find someone to couple up and stay at home with? Where, I wonder, are the girls?

I find them on a weekend trip to London. At this time, Candy Bar is the most famous lesbian venue in the capital, possibly the country. Nestled in a side street in Soho, outside there's a neon sign and a gaggle of women. I'm hoping for a sapphic Cheers vibe, where all the lesbians know your name and they're always glad you came. The atmosphere I walk into isn't quite so cosy.

Robyn and I order our drinks and sit on the banquette seats, clutching our glasses. I glance around nervously. There are other women in here, but they all seem to know each other already and sit in cliques. I was so excited about coming to a lesbian bar as part of a lesbian couple and being surrounded by other lesbians, but now I'm here I feel strangely out of place.

Maybe I'm being paranoid, but I feel like there's tension in the air. There is *a lot* of loaded staring. Everyone seems to be sussing each other out. I feel intimidated. They all seem so unapproachable. This isn't the warm, welcoming embrace I was hoping for. It's an odd experience, knowing that there is a scene for people like me, actually being right here in the heart of that scene, yet still not feeling part of it. At least not yet.

We keep to ourselves and as the evening goes on, the place fills up and becomes friendlier. Lubricated by alcohol, everyone loosens up. They stop being stand-offish and start being smiley.

We head to the basement, where we're swept up in a sea of excited sapphics. Pink is blasting on the sound system. It's hot, cramped and sweaty, but I don't care. I am soaring and it isn't just the booze. It's the visceral experience of being here in this lesbian physical space. I am riding so high right now, lifted by the energy of this glorious collective. This feels euphoric, magnificent, moving. Looking around at all these joyous, liberated women who are just like me, I literally can't wipe the beam from my face.

❖

Despite being an institution, Candy Bar goes on to close its doors permanently in 2014, adding one more name to the long list of queer spaces that are shutting down. A 2017 report by the UK government shows that London lost 58 per cent of its LGBTQIA spaces in the previous decade. Over in America, The Lesbian Bar Project charts the decline of lesbian bars, from around two hundred across the US in the 1980s, to fewer than thirty in 2023. There are many theories about why so many LGBTQIA spaces are closing. There are those who claim lesbian spaces can't survive because they believe that lesbians don't go out or spend money and, essentially, we just want to hang out at home with our cats. Now I admit that hanging out at home with cats does sound appealing, but so does cutting loose at a lesbian bar, out on the town with my community.

There's also this notion that queer spaces in general are no longer necessary, that due to greater acceptance in the mainstream, we don't need to go to special venues to feel safe. While it's true that there's more queer visibility than ever, I'm sceptical about the suggestion that the need for our own spaces has gone. We know visibility is vital, but visibility can also bring vulnerability. When the spotlight is shone on a marginalized identity, there can be backlash, hatred and violence. In 2023 LGBT+ anti-abuse charity Galop reported a 65 per cent increase in LGBTQIA victims of hate crime seeking their support in the previous year alone. Official government statistics confirm that homophobic and transphobic hate crime is still alarmingly high. So no, the need for safe, inclusive LGBTQIA nightlife has not conveniently vanished.

I suspect that the real reason for the decline of queer bars has a lot more to do with money. That's why Candy Bar closed. Increasing gentrification means rocketing rent prices, pushing many marginalized communities out of the spaces they previously occupied.

It is sad to see our spaces close their doors one by one, to remember the wild nights we had there, that feeling of togetherness, the frisson of flirting and drinking and celebrating in a bar just for us. But I'm hopeful for the future of queer nightlife, and no, I'm not drunk while I'm writing this.

I'm hopeful because despite widespread reports of 'the death of the lesbian bar', there are resilient sapphic spaces bucking this trend. Spaces like Manchester's Vanilla, which opened in 1998, and Soho's She Bar, serving sapphics since 2014.

In 2024 the community is fizzing with the news that a brand new inclusive lesbian bar is launching in Hackney. On opening night, La Camionera (which is Spanish slang for butch lesbian) attracts literally hundreds of thirsty queer women and non-binary people, immediately going viral on social media. When I visit, it's buzzing. The sapphics have been waiting for something like this. With its Mediterranean aesthetic and beer garden, it feels intimate and laidback, casually sexy and very cool.

And then there are flourishing, long-running nights like Gal Pals, Pxssy Palace and Butch, Please! Plus new ones popping up all the time: Strapped, WET, Magic Dyke and more. In fact, there are so many new events in 2024, it's dubbed the year of the dyke renaissance.

As queer people, we adapt, we regenerate and we find new ways to gather and form community. I believe that there is still hope for the magic of a dancefloor filled with sweaty, queer bodies. The party is far from over.

❀

Back in 2008, the party is only just getting started. I save up my meagre call centre wages and splash out on a ticket to Oz. After my parents weren't exactly thrilled by my big gay announcement, it seems like the next logical step to board a plane bound for the other side of the planet. So Robyn and I are going on tour. The plane journey technically lasts 24 hours, but it feels like it's taken me a lifetime to get here.

A letter from my granny

Dearest Roxana

Wishing you happiness and success on your journey.

I know you have a lot of courage and inner strength to overcome any sagas which may occur. I have enjoyed so much the philosophical chats we have had over the years, and been impressed by your maturity.

I certainly wish for all that is good to happen for you. I am very proud of you.

Keep smiling, and always remember, you are very much loved, and precious to us folks at home.

So – look after yourself. I'll be thinking of you every day.

Sending all my love

Granny

xx

CHAPTER 9

Rainbow glitter! Drag queens! DYKES ON BIKES!!

Glitter billows in the breeze. Camp anthems pump into the sky. I have arrived in Sydney, just in time for Mardi Gras. The day after my flight touches down, I am at my very first Pride parade. For this one extraordinary day, everything is topsy-turvy and queer people are the majority.

Standing in the middle of Sydney's gaybourhood, in the centre of Oxford Street near the Stonewall Hotel, I am surrounded by literally hundreds of thousands of LGBTQIA folks, all of them beaming and cheering and dancing for the gods. The sun is shining, the drag queens are singing. The whole of this historic high street, affectionately known as 'the gay golden mile', is crammed with party people, all here to watch the parade and celebrate Pride. This is a salve for the soul. After all the angst of the past few years, today is my panacea. The antidote to all that private agony of feeling like a freak. If I'm a freak, today the freaks are in charge. A queer collective, we take over the whole city with our defiant explosion of joy.

Suddenly I hear the roar of a hundred engines and a hundred lesbians. Oh wow, it's the Dykes on Bikes. Riding right through the heart of the city, they straddle colossal motorbikes between their thighs, revving for their lives. Some ride solo, others with their girlfriends' arms wrapped around their waists. Many wear leather jackets emblazoned with Pride flag patches. A couple are completely topless, save for two precarious slivers of gaffer tape. A few appear incredibly casual, almost nonchalant, as if they are on their way to do the weekly shop rather than at the front of one of the biggest Pride parades in the world. My favourites are the ones who really put some welly into it, all empowered with their fists raised up, high on the crowd's ecstatic cheers.

The Dykes on Bikes are instantly iconic, but they're only the start of the celebrations. There is so much to see and I soak it all up. Flamboyantly dressed gays performing carefully choreographed dance routines. Determined marchers brandishing DIY placards demanding 'LEGALIZE GAY MARRIAGE' and 'END BIPHOBIA NOW!' And would you look at that? Here comes the Mature Age Gays bus, full of pensioners decked out in matching glittery pink jumpers, waving warmly at us all. Oh, and here are the Rainbow Kids with their LGBTQIA parents. A little girl runs over to give me a high five and wish me a 'Happy Mardi Gras!' A grinning teenage boy strides along wearing a T-shirt with a message in bold on the back: 'I'M NOT GAY BUT MY MOMS ARE'. He walks hand in hand with his aforementioned moms. A sparkly mermaid sits slouched in a giant clam shell, as they are carried aloft, their face incongruously deadpan despite the merriment of the crowd.

Time for a quick herstory lesson. Pride began as a riot. In New York in 1969, police raided Greenwich Village gay bar The Stonewall Inn and hundreds of LGBTQIA people fought back, tired of being targeted because of their identities. Among them were trailblazing lesbian, queer and trans people of colour, like Marsha P. Johnson, Sylvia Rivera and Stormé DeLarverie. After the riots ended, the first Christopher Street Liberation Day march took place, organized by the brilliant, bisexual 'Mother of Pride' Brenda Howard. Over the following years, Pride marches sprang up across Europe and the US, with the first London Pride held in 1972 when the Gay Liberation Front marched through the capital.

So Pride is, at heart, not just a party but also a protest, not just revelry but also rage. It is both a mammoth display of empowering joy and a rallying cry for urgent action. We must not forget that urgent action part because more than fifty years after it all began, there is still a hell of a lot to be angry about. Progress is not linear and rights, as we have bitterly learned, cannot be taken for granted. People might think things are better for the LGBTQIA community now, and in some ways they are, but in so many ways there is still so much further to go. And there is also still power, healing, emboldening power, in being surrounded by people like you, and publicly celebrating the very thing we have been conditioned to feel ashamed of.

Pride is what we do to prove to ourselves and everyone else that we are not alone. Pride is the medicine we take to soothe away the torment of a lifetime spent being othered. I love that we can experience this euphoria in June, but I can't help wondering, what about the rest of the year? Don't we deserve to live in a world where we feel liberated to be ourselves every single day, not just on special occasions?

When I move to Sydney, I attempt to create such an existence. Maybe I'm making up for lost time or experiencing a kind of second adolescence. Like so many before me, I come out of the closet and dive tits deep into everything gay I can find.

So far away from home, I submerge myself in the sapphic. We rent a room in a shared house in the gaybourhood. I start coming out to every new person I encounter: 'Hi, I'm a homosexual, great to meet you.' I am up for any activity as long as it is prefixed by the word 'gay'. I spend hours browsing the gay bookshop, going to gay drag queen bingo and sunbathing on the gay beach.

In Sydney there is a whole scene with loads of different lesbian nights, and I am excited at the prospect of being part of it. Compared to the scene I left behind in Leeds, it seems like there's so much more going on here for the girls. We go to a lesbian night called Bitch and see Ruby Rose DJ. We spend weekends hanging out in Newtown, which I'm told is one of the lesbian districts. ONE OF! There's also Leichhardt, AKA Dykeheart. In Newtown, Robyn and I walk down the street holding hands, relaxed and leisurely, not bracing ourselves in pre-emptive fear of unwanted remarks or abuse. It is such a simple pleasure that I have never felt before and I savour it. I marvel at it. I can't quite believe that there's a whole part of town so full of mohawked lesbian couples strolling down the pavement and bands of lesbifriends overflowing out of coffee shop windows.

❉

There is something sapphic in the air. It's the late noughties and 'lesbian chic' is having a moment. The same year I move to Sydney and attend my first Pride, Katy Perry's 'I Kissed a Girl' is released. Every lesbian night plays it and when the song comes on, the dancefloor floods with geed-up queers. Later on, Katy Perry's song will be critiqued for its problematic depiction of bisexuality, but right now I am singing along to it with gusto with all the other women in the club. It feels cheeky, transgressive and, most of all, communal. We suddenly have this shared cultural reference point we can all play with together. There is an undeniable thrill in being in a crowd of sapphics and belting out those words as one: 'I kissed a girl and I liked it'.

It's a strange double-sided thing when your identity is suddenly in vogue. There's no doubt that it is exciting to see yourself represented, to notice mainstream magazines talking about queer stuff and sing along to lesbionic lyrics on nights out. At various times 'lesbian chic' or 'queer cool' have been hailed as the height of fashion. In the 1990s, out lesbian singer k.d. lang appears on the cover of *Vanity Fair* being shaved by supermodel Cindy Crawford, and Madonna frolics with butches in her video for 'Erotica'. In the noughties, songs like 'I Kissed a Girl' and t.A.T.u.'s 'All The Things She Said' storm the charts, and Madge is at it again, onstage at the VMAs participating in a three-way-snog with Britney Spears and Christina Aguilera.

But being chic isn't the same as having fair and equal treatment. The mainstream media that runs titillating articles about the rise of 'lesbian chic' also outs celebrities against their will. The same year as the VMAs popstar multi-snog, UK broadcaster Clare Balding is outed by *The Mail on Sunday*. She had been keeping quiet about her sexuality, fearing if she didn't it would harm her career. As she shares in an interview on *Desert Island Discs* years later, although her parents already knew she was gay, her grandmother didn't. After the story broke, they didn't speak for six months, which Clare describes to journalist Kirsty Young as 'difficult'.

Plus the whole idea that my sexual orientation, a key part of my identity, can be commodified as a fashion trend is unsettling. There's something very clearly disposable about it: 'Hey consumer, why not accessorize your outfit with these cool sunglasses and a vague suggestion of homosexuality?' If something can be in fashion, it can also be out of fashion, but queerness is not a fad. I'm still going to be a lesbian when 'lesbian chic' goes out of style, just as I'm still going to be gay when all the rainbow glitter of Pride has washed away down the drain.

✽

'Save a lollipop – suck a dick!' These are the words rendered in lurid spray paint across the camper van in front of us. Robyn and I had thought that hiring a low-budget motor home for a coastal roadtrip was a genius idea. We had thought it would be romantic. Just the two of us and the open road. And our offensively graffitied abomination.

There are so many offensively graffitied abominations at the collection point to choose from. Or rather, not choose from. We have no say whatsoever in which monstrosity will be our home for the next month. What will our roadtrip motto be? 'Drink til she's pretty'? 'Life sucks if your girlfriend doesn't'? God, I hope we don't get 'Virginity is curable'.

This flippantly misogynist 'banter' is typical of the time. The late noughties mark not only the trend for 'lesbian chic' but also the peak of 'lad-culture'. The so-called jokes scrawled all over these shoddy-looking vans echo the tone of popular lad-mags like *Loaded*, *Nuts* and *Zoo*. I would like to clarify that we have not gone for this particular company because of their chauvinist designs. We chose them purely because they were the cheapest. But now, our romantic roadtrip fantasy is starting to look very different indeed.

In the end our designated vehicle is decorated with a cartoon portrait of a stoner, along with the inexplicable tagline, 'Armageddon? Bullshit!' Although actually, catastrophic visions of the end of humanity sound about right for the trip we're about to embark on. Not only is our ignoble steed butt ugly, it looks like it might fall apart at any moment. Is this beaten-up old wreck even roadworthy? I guess it's time to find out!

I really don't want to get inside this thing. Partly because it looks like it could spontaneously combust at any moment. Mostly because anyone who sees us in it will assume, quite reasonably, that we are absolute knobs with zero manners and even less taste. Look out, here come the yobs on tour.

Still, it could be worse. I watch on with pity as a dad and daughter duo are allocated a van covered in stick figure diagrams of sex positions. They board in crestfallen silence.

I peer inside Armageddon doubtfully. The front seat is filthy with frayed seatbelts. In the back are our sleeping quarters for the next four weeks, consisting of a stained, skimpy mattress with scabby-looking blankets. I sniff the air dubiously, detecting a distinctly musty aroma. Nevertheless, we clamber inside and exchange a pained look that communicates, 'Oh shit, what have we done?' Then Robyn cranks the stiff gears into squeaky life.

As we set off from Cairns, the celebrated Sunshine Coast is barraged with tropical storms and torrential rainfall. In a desperate attempt to outrun the rain, we bomb down the Bruce Highway and cover most of Queensland's coastline in a couple of days. At night, we attempt to sleep in our poky makeshift bed, as rain leaks through the roof.

After a few days on the road, we're so dishevelled and knackered we impulsively check into a hotel for the night. Armageddon looks ludicrously out of place in the car park. So much so that a holidaymaker takes pity on us and anonymously leaves a food parcel on the bumper. There are jars of preservatives, olive oil and a pineapple, along with a handwritten note saying sympathetically 'Hope this helps'. We are touched by this stranger's random act of kindness.

Despite the rocky start, among the rubble of our roadtrip we do find moments of bliss. One day the sun decides to shine, so we cruise along the highway with the windows wound down, our music on full blast. My feet are up on the dashboard and Robyn's arm is draped around my shoulder. There's not another soul in sight. We stumble across a deserted sandy beach and paddle with the whole place to ourselves. It's a glimmer of paradise.

A few weeks after we drop off Armageddon, I see a news report about complaints against the camper van company. Disgruntled customers describe the vehicles they rented as 'death traps'. I am not surprised, but I am relieved we survived.

You'd think our very own Armageddon experience would put us off pursuing other zany backpacker adventures. It doesn't.

Spending three months working on a gay nudist farm seems like a good idea at the time. Sure, farming while starkers poses considerable health and safety risks, but just think of how tanned we'll be! So, this is why we are heading to a remote location in rural Australia to labour over the land as fruit pickers, AKA WWOOFers.

WWOOFing is where people, typically backpackers, volunteer their time as farmhands in exchange for a second year visa. Robyn is keen for us to stay in Oz for as long as possible before we return to the UK, and she's heard about this farm that sounds perfect. Neither of us are nudists. But we're worried we might be met with animosity in the Aussie countryside. One time in Queensland, we were strolling down the street together, when we clocked locals looking at us with pure homophobic hostility in their eyes. One woman found our existence so offensive and morally corrupt, she literally shielded her child's eyes from seeing us. But we figure this gay nudist farm sounds like a safe bet, suitably liberal and inclusive. I'm picturing a sunny utopia of friendly, naked queer folks of all kinds. We're confident we'll fit right in. A couple of dykes with hoes.

We arrive at the tiny local airport and watch nervously as all the other passengers leave. Where's our ride? Are we stranded in the Outback? At long last, a dusty four-wheel-drive rolls up and a frail, elderly man shuffles out. He's the farm's longest-serving WWOOFer, the only WWOOFer WWOOFing right now apart from us, and an enthusiastic nudist. He takes it for granted that we are too. To be fair, why wouldn't he? We are the non-nudist imbeciles at the nudist farm.

He invites us to join him for a nudist dinner party. And hey, if we weren't the only guests, we'd probably have said sure. When on a nudist farm, be nude. We may well have had a jolly, jiggly time, as long as we didn't spill anything piping hot on our intimate areas. But the prospect of a naked soiree with just us and him feels a tad intense, so we politely decline his offer of an unerotic, non-sexual three-way with hors d'oeuvres.

When we arrive at the farm, we meet the farmer's lodger. He is the slimiest of slimeballs. Always there, always creepy. He keeps trying to show us pictures of women he's slept with. The first time it happens I foolishly assume I'm going to see a smiley headshot. Instead, he thrusts his phone in front of my eyes and I'm greeted with a full-frontal close-up of his conquest's nether regions.

Back in our room on the first night, tanned but terrified, we're summoned into the lounge by the lecherous lodger. We enter with caution. What does he want with us? I hope it's not another round of snatch show-and-tell. He starts filming with his mobile phone, ordering us to kiss for the camera. We refuse and run back to our room. We do not feel safe. We're supposed to be staying for three months, but by the end of the week we've scarpered back to Sydney. It was never like this on *Neighbours*.

✻

Now it's a sunny day in late November 2009, but we are not barbequing on Bronte Beach, sunbathing in the Botanical Gardens or grabbing a cocktail on Oxford Street, as we often do at the weekend. Instead, we are standing outside the town hall among the crowds. We are here because the Australian campaign for marriage equality has announced A National Year of Action. Same-sex marriage is not legal here at this time. Homosexuality was only decriminalized in New South Wales in 1984, and it was still illegal in Tasmania until 1997. In an effort to bring marriage equality into being, major cities around the country are holding rallies, and we're at one of them right now.

I can see rainbow flags, placards declaring, 'My love, your love, same love' and 'Who do you think designs your wedding dresses?' I smile when I spot two women in coordinating ivory outfits, one in a trouser suit, the other in a wedding gown. We listen rapt to powerful speeches about LGBTQIA rights. We watch the illegal mass queer wedding ceremony. Same-sex couples are presented with red roses. The reverend gives a solemn speech. Then they all kiss and fling their flowers in the air as the 'Bridal Chorus' plays on full blast.

It's uplifting, but we're also aware that not everyone here is on our side. A right-wing Christian group called Salt Shakers has come to oppose us. Two days ago, we saw on Facebook that they were planning to get photo evidence to undermine the event, taking misleading pictures to make it look like barely anyone showed up. It made us even more determined to attend.

It's swelteringly hot, but that's not going to stop us and neither are the homophobes. As we march through the centre of the city, Robyn and I hold our clasped hands high in the air. We join in with the chants: 'What do we want? Equal marriage! When do we want it? Now!' People in their cars toot their horns in support. The atmosphere is amazing. My emotions are running high. When a guy from a local TV station thrusts a camera in front of my face and asks me why I am marching, I find myself giving an impassioned speech about us just wanting the same rights everyone else takes for granted.

In eight years' time I will read the news that Australia has finally legalized same-sex marriage. I will know I am supposed to feel happy about this, that the thing I was campaigning for has finally happened. But happiness won't be my first reaction. Of course, I will think it is a good thing that this law has passed. Of course, I will be grateful for the campaigners who made this happen through their tireless, sustained activism. But when I look at the results of the public postal vote, my honest emotional response will be anger.

I will be angry that this issue was ever put to a public vote. I will be grateful to the 62 per cent who voted for same-sex marriage, but I won't be able to stop thinking about the 38 per cent who voted against. That's almost four out of ten people, who made an active decision to try and block the basic rights of my community. I will be furious that they have been allowed a say. I don't recall being asked to vote on whether straight couples should be permitted the right to marry. It will serve as a stark reminder that LGBTQIA people are so often treated as second class citizens. Other people's rights are by default, our rights are up for debate.

But all that righteous anger is in the future. For today at this rally in 2009, I don't feel rageful. I feel defiant and optimistic. I am holding my girlfriend's hand up high for all to see in the dazzling Sydney sunshine. I am galvanized by being part of a queer collective on a mission. I am hopeful for a brighter tomorrow.

Ten lessons I've learned about Pride

1. You will get glitter wedged in crevices you did not know you had.
2. There is no such thing as overdressed at Pride. No matter how outrageously flamboyant you believe your outfit to be, you will always be upstaged two minutes later by a drag queen dressed as a unicorn on stilts.
3. It's good to come up with a game plan, ahead of time, for how you're going to tackle the day. Once you're at Pride this will inevitably go completely out of the window as you get swept up in all the madness, but for a while it will give you a comforting, albeit false, sense of security.
4. It is very likely you will lose track of your friends. A good way to avoid this is to spend the weeks leading up to Pride strategically befriending especially tall people. A great place to find them is at your local drag bar.
5. The big day itself can be a lot, but try and keep an upbeat, positive attitude. Party poopers are about as welcome at Pride as a surprise fart at a job interview.
6. Stay hydrated. That means sipping water, not knocking back another round of Slippery Nipples. If you're drinking alcohol, aim for merrily squiffy, not biblically slaughtered. If you're tee-total, you're about to find out what utter nincompoops drunk people can be.

7. High-five people who are in the parade. They bloody love it. It's like the queer secret handshake, only easy to remember and not in the least bit secret.

8. There are certain people you will undoubtedly encounter at Pride. One of these is The Wasted Girl. Be kind to The Wasted Girl. We have all been The Wasted Girl. Just don't get too close or she'll up-chuck on your shoes.

9. You will also inevitably encounter the anti-Pride protesters. These guys aren't protesting for important causes like bi visibility, intersex rights or IVF equality for same-sex couples. No. They are protesting Pride itself because happy queer people really grind their gears. You can easily spot them because they invariably look miserable and carry placards saying things like 'God hates fags' and 'It's Adam and Eve, not Adam and Steve!' These guys come every year. They are clearly big fans. You have three options for how to handle them. Option a: ignore them completely, pretend you literally cannot see them and just carry on being awesome regardless. Option b: let them know what you think of them, e.g. a bit of light booing, politely suggesting they 'get a life', or if you're feeling bold, flipping the bird. Or, my personal favourite, option c: bamboozle these ill-wishers by welcoming them warmly, 'Hey, it's you guys again! Happy Pride, you guys!' I like to bust out my most extravagant, joyful dance moves especially for them with a great big smile on my face. They did wait an awfully long time in the rain for their front row seats, after all.

10. At some point during the day you will have an

epiphany. You will feel overwhelmed by love, community and queer joy. You will weep sparkly tears and those sparkly tears will decimate that rainbow stripy make-up you thought was a good idea at the time. It will be worth it. Feel all your feelings, completely fuck-up your face paint, and remember the power and poignancy of this moment right now.

CHAPTER 10

The Clothes

Something strange happens when I finally come out of the closet. I promptly reach back into it and throw out all my favourite clothes.

At the time, I tell myself this is an act of liberation. I've seen enough lifestyle TV shows to believe that decluttering is a fast-track to catharsis and self-improvement. I am purging the past so I can start afresh. I am unburdening myself of surplus worldly possessions and only holding onto items I truly need, all of which must fit inside the four-foot-tall backpack I'm hauling to Australia. I am ridding my childhood home of my piles of stuff, cutting all those material ties to somehow set myself free. It is, in fact, a huge mistake.

A lot of queer women talk about growing up as 'a tomboy', playing sports, having mostly male friends and feeling uncomfortable, even dysphoric, in dresses. That was never me. I was extraordinarily bad at anything athletic and when my head wasn't stuck in a book, I was making my dolls fall in love with each other and being extremely, stereotypically 'girly'. I like pink, so sue me. To clarify on the girly front, I never wanted to faff about with pretend cookers or hoover up imaginary dust with fake vacuum cleaners. I wasn't interested in toys from the girls' section that glorified the drudgery of housework, but I was enchanted by Barbie and her never-ending wardrobe. She always had the perfect ensemble for every activity. She could be a gymnast, a scientist, a pop star, a mermaid or anything else I could imagine if she had The Clothes.

My beloved granny was the most radiant beauty I had ever seen in real life and she adored The Clothes just as much as I did. Always spectacularly, thoughtfully dressed, she wore coordinated outfits that she designed and sewed herself. She never left the house without her lipstick and powder compact. As a child I would sit spellbound on the end of her bed, watching her brushing her hair at her antique dressing table with her three-way mirror and know her to be the last word in glamour. We talked about The Clothes endlessly. She told me about her mother, who had been a flapper doing the Charleston in frocks with frills. We gossiped about the gowns worn by Old Hollywood movie stars like Greta Garbo and Jean Harlow. I quizzed her for vintage beauty tips (drink hot water with lemon and put Vaseline on your eyelashes). She showed me old black and white photographs of herself as a young woman, in flowery frocks, tailored skirt suits and strapless satin evening dresses accessorized with dangling earrings. We pored over fashion spreads in magazines together, discussing our precise opinions on the merits of the cut of this skirt, the embellishment on that jacket. I was enamoured by her and by it all. The Clothes were our shared hobby. I knew that when I grew up, I wanted to be an impossibly glamorous, witty, charming lady like Granny.

My budding devotion to style didn't stop there. I used to spend hours drawing paper dolls and sketching hundreds of two-dimensional outfits, all with little tabs I could fold over to 'dress them' up in different looks. I would scrutinize the costumes worn on TV shows and marvel at how each outfit helped tell the story of exactly who that character was. I was fascinated by the semiotics of clothing. To me, The Clothes were not superficial. They were emotional and transformative. I never bothered much with trends or what was 'in'. I cared about the creativity of clothes, the promise of the perfect outfit and the eternal quest to find a signature look, that said who you were while making you feel more yourself.

The Clothes were a portal to another realm of wonder. I gravitated towards styles from the past, like the ones in the pictures Granny had shown me, and I felt nostalgia for a time before I was born. Clothes that had already lived a secret life fired my imagination and filled me with awe. From the age of twelve I always had a part-time job to fund my sartorial habit. I was a thrifty shopper and an early adopter of eBay. I scoured second-hand stores and charity shops and vintage emporiums, hunting for treasures that made my heart soar.

By the time I hit my twenties my wardrobe was bursting with colour and drama and preposterous glamour way out of proportion to my actual lifestyle, but I did not care. I was so in love with The Clothes. I craved 1950s candy-coloured prom dresses with nipped-in waists and petticoats, 1940s ladylike box handbags with intricate embroidery, 1920s velvet wraps in jewel tones edged with fringing. My love language was sumptuous fabrics, striking shades and defined silhouettes. I hated my body, but I loved the way clothes could play down the parts I was most self-conscious about and distract me from my self-perceived flaws with all that fabulousness. I decided I wanted to dress like the leading lady of my own life in the manner of a mid-century movie star, although perhaps one who has let herself go a bit in between films. The Clothes were how I conveyed myself to the world and found magic in the everyday. The Clothes were my passion, my creative self-expression and my single-minded obsession.

And then I come out. Then I come out and announce my lesbian self. This should be the moment I am standing in my truth and fully expressing my whole authentic being to the world, but I make a critical mistake. The rush of my new love distracts me from my first love, The Clothes. Of course, it's not just about losing sight of The Clothes. It's about losing sight of myself, the things that bring me joy and express who I am.

I start dressing differently. This is partly to do with wanting to look less out of place on the scene. I am, in my misguided way, trying to look more like 'a real lesbian'. I have come out, but now all I want to do is fit in. I want to feel accepted by the lesbians I see on the scene and they do not wear glamorous dresses. They wear, almost without exception, jeans. Many of them have short hair. I briefly consider getting mine chopped, but worry that I don't have the bone structure to pull this off.

Here I am wearing a checked shirt, skinny jeans and no lipstick. I might look more like I belong in this gay bar, but I don't feel comfortable at all. I feel ugly and wrong and not like myself. I notice how people respond differently to me. They seem less sceptical and more welcoming. Sure, I'm glad to be included, but I'm also disappointed that this is what it took. I was just as gay in my flowery frock.

With this new more casual style, I am also trying to look like Robyn's dream woman. A child of the 1990s, I am a firm believer in the power of a makeover, so I give myself a make-over to try and transform into her ideal girl.

She's told me she usually goes for slim women, she's never been into big boobs and she loves cool-looking indie girls in short denim skirts. So that is what I – curvy with massive tits and a devotion to vintage glamour – try and emulate. I start wearing baggy T-shirts and tight minis. Robyn loves rock music. She has pierced eyebrows and studs in her nose.

I get my lip pierced. I've always been at war with my body, always felt it was too much, too unruly with too many wobbly bits. And now I'm with someone who I know fancies me, but I also know I am not her usual type. I start going jogging with her. I am not my best self when I am jogging. I am very bad at it and I hate it, but I yearn to be thinner.

The wardrobe clear-out happens partly because I am aware that The Clothes I have amassed do not fit in with my recent makeover. Rummaging through my collection of brightly coloured vintage dresses and slightly battered second-hand handbags, Robyn thinks a lot of it is, well, a little bit silly. I have not told her what The Clothes mean to me. She does not know that when she laughs at an ancient dress and calls it ridiculous, it feels like she is saying that I am ridiculous for ever loving and wearing and being moved by that dress. But how could she know that? I, in my lovedrunk haze and desperation to be her dream girl personified, tell her I agree. I betray The Clothes. Please forgive me, Clothes. I shove my treasured, precious, painstakingly curated wardrobe into black bin bags and cart them off back to the charity shop they came from. She doesn't make me do this. I choose to do this. It is my decision, but it is a bad decision. I will go on to mourn those clothes more than I mourn some of my past relationships. (Side note – if anyone stumbled across a cerise, rose-print, 1950s halter neck dress in the early noughties in a charity shop in Leeds, please alert the authorities, i.e. me.)

❀

Years later, I am now fully back to embracing my inner high femme. I no longer suppress my most authentic self to please a partner or try and fit into a community that is supposed to be all about being who you really are. I have replenished my wardrobe of vintage treasures and, through extensive trial-and-error, discovered my dream shade of scarlet lipstick. It pays homage to Old Hollywood glam and doesn't make my teeth look yellow. I rarely leave the house without two coats of Max Factor's Ruby Tuesday, which is even more dreamy because it shares its name with a legendary London lesbian party. This is the kind of detail-oriented, nostalgic, playful manifestation of style that makes me swoon.

It's odd that anyone would think that these two passions of mine – vintage style and seducing women – are mutually exclusive, but they do. I've had strangers mistakenly assume that me dressing in 'traditional' clothing goes hand in hand with me conforming to 'traditional' ideas about gender and sexuality. They imagine that dressing like I'm from the 1950s means I want to actually live in the 1950s, a time when misogyny was normalized, male homosexuality was criminalized and lesbianism was stigmatized. To them I say, I channel old-fashioned elegance, not old-fashioned values, and the only thing I want oppressed is my waistline, preferably in a fetching satin cincher.

For huge swathes of the LGBTQIA community terms like butch and femme have absolutely no relevance to their lives or identities. They don't feel any connection to those words. But for me, claiming the word femme is a powerful assertion that despite what I've been told by both straight and queer people, my love of traditional 'femininity' in no way diminishes my love of women.

I also love the history of these words. I love that way back in the early twentieth century our community invented them to communicate our ways of being. I love that these identities are a queer creation, not, as some might think, an aping of heterosexuality. I love hearing stories about The Gateways, London's notorious lesbian bar that ran from the 1940s to 1985, where butches and femmes reigned supreme. And I really love imagining that bustling lesbian bar filled with Brylcreemed butches in the shiniest of shoes, and femmes with their glamorous frocks and black handbags.

Of course, nobody should feel they have to look a certain way to be accepted as LGBTQIA. That's the whole point, isn't it? Be your truest, most authentic self, whatever that looks like, however feels best for you. For me, I tried eschewing the creative glamour I'd always gravitated towards. I attempted to look more androgynous, cooler, 'gayer'. It felt horribly inauthentic and it made me sad, because I was denying myself a world of pleasure. I was trying to be someone I just wasn't.

If I'm feeling grandiose, I like to imagine that embracing vintage femme glamour connects me not only with my dazzling granny, but also with the silver screen femmes of yesteryear. Femmes like Tallulah Bankhead, the bisexual starlet rumoured to have romanced a long list of prominent women of her time, from Marlene Dietrich to Hattie McDaniel. My kind of queer icon, she called everyone 'dah-ling', regularly cartwheeled into parties with no knickers on and had a pet parakeet named Gaylord.

Of course, in many ways how I dress has little to do with my sexuality. On the one hand, I am reclaiming my queer femininity outside heteronormativity and honouring my femme foremothers. On the other hand, I just love sparkles. Pretty things lift my spirits. By consistently trying to look as fabulous as I can, I imbue each day with a sense of possibility. Who knows where this day and this outfit will take me? Permanently overdressed, I am always ready for a last-minute ball invite. Also, I just find being really into The Clothes makes life so much more fun. Everyday existence can be mundane and miserable. Why not grab every opportunity for happiness?

❦

Tonight, I am on my way to a very exciting event. I have recently started working at *DIVA* and I'm out on an assignment, covering a queer fashion show. I am very excited about this. I love being queer and I love fashion. I figure that this occasion calls for a fabulous look, so I am decked out in a stunning 1950s emerald pencil dress, high heels and seamed stockings. My hair is meticulously curled and my lips are smothered in Ruby Tuesday.

I arrive at the venue and I'm delighted to find crowds of queers wearing jaw-dropping outfits. The vibe is creative, eclectic and full of self-expression through style. There is face paint and lots of leather and mullets dyed primary colours, women rocking androgynous suits and genderfluid Bowie-esque beings in assless chaps. I'm beaming away at all the epic ensembles and gushing over how gorgeous and free everyone is.

We are ushered into a cavernous room and the show begins. On a huge screen an image of Marilyn Monroe appears. A model with old school blonde curls and bright red lips struts down the runway. When the model reaches the end, they whip their wig off, defiantly revealing their shaved head. They raise one arm up and smudge the lipstick right across their face, so it leaves an angry crimson blur. As the crowd cheers at this metaphorical 'fuck you' to these symbols of 'traditional femininity', I stand among them, withering in humiliation, a fool with ringlets and red lipstick.

I get what they're doing. I get the queer punk anarchy vibe and the power that can be found in rejecting gender norms. I get the statement they're making and the audience around me is lapping it up. But I also feel publicly roasted. I have accidently come dressed as the very thing they are mocking.

Is everyone looking or am I being paranoid? Oh god, are those people laughing at me? Do they think I'm part of the show? Are they waiting for me to theatrically smear off my own make-up, muss up my hair and tear apart my lovely dress?

I am all for people embracing their authentic selves, but surely this can be achieved without making others feel belittled. The outfit I was so delighted with, which felt like such a fun, empowering expression of my femme, lesbian, vintage-loving, glamourpuss self, now feels like a giant siren blaring out a shameful message for all these queer fashion aficionados to see: 'not one of us, not really queer'. I had mistakenly assumed I was in a safe space.

This is just one of the many times I feel weird about my femmeness in a queer community setting. As a cis, white, femme woman I am aware I have a huge amount of privilege in society. I am also aware that I am sometimes treated differently because of the way I look, that my femmeness can be taken for weakness, and that when this happens at the hands of members of my own community there is a particular pang of injustice and feeling misunderstood.

There are times when I am treated in the same way by a group of queer people as I have been in the past by certain straight men. Because of my appearance, I am sometimes taken less seriously than butcher women, assumed to be slightly dimmer, a bit vacuous, occasionally treated as 'the totty'. They talk grown-up talk with each other as if I am not there, aside from the odd gawk at my chest.

It can sometimes feel like there is a hierarchy of queerness and femmes are lower down the pecking order. Maybe it's the gay version of old-fashioned misogyny, the belief that our perceived 'femininity' is innately lesser than, less serious, less valid, less authentically queer. Buying into this idea is buying into the same sexist bullshit that's been screwing women over for centuries. It can absolutely be empowering to embrace a particular gender non-conforming aesthetic, but we also need to hold space for LGBTQIA people to express themselves in whatever way feels good for them, without judgement.

It is a sad moment when I realize that just because we're queer, doesn't mean we're perfect. I had hoped that the sapphic community would be an idyll like Wonder Woman's Island, with equal pay for all and loads of lovely consensual snogging. But misogyny still exists in the LGBTQIA landscape, just as it does in the straight world. It's one of the reasons why so many queer spaces are still dominated by gay men, but it's also why, even in those spaces filled with gay women, equality is not a given. We've all been subjected to the insidious mechanisms of the patriarchy and the routine objectification of women, yet some of us still do it to each other. Toxic masculinity is still very much a thing. Just because a woman fancies other women, that does not automatically guarantee that she cares one bit about the rights of her objects of lust.

Perhaps the lingering prejudice against femmes is because of an assumption that we are pandering to the male gaze. But my love of style in no way diminishes my love of women and the queer community. Wearing a pencil skirt and heels doesn't stop me from trampling all over the patriarchy. And I do not dress for men; I dress for me. If I'm dressing for anyone other than me, it is for other women, specifically those under the age of ten and over the age of seventy. I dress for the girl on the tube who sees my glamorous get-up and tugs at her mum's hemline, pointing and whispering, 'Is she a princess?' making me glow with admittedly slightly smug pride. I dress for the stylish OAP in a cashmere scarf who crosses the street to enquire where I nabbed my beaded pastel cardigan. I dress for my granny, because she taught me how to truly love The

Clothes and I long to be one iota as stylish and stunning as her. Caring about clothes does not stop me from caring about equal rights. I care greatly about the world and its people, but I also find creativity, enchantment and a deeper connection to myself through The Clothes. I think this is something to be celebrated, not sneered at.

We need to make space for all of us, however we present. We need to uplift each other, whether we are butch or femme or anything in between or none of the above. At the bare minimum, we must show each other that we are all worthy of respect. Let's not propagate the kind of misogyny that judges a woman on how she looks.

The new rules of style

1. There are no rules of style. The title of this page is ironic and, admittedly, misleading. Sorry about that.
2. Ok, you really want a rule? How about this for a rule? Wear whatever the hell you want!
3. Seriously, whether you're LGBTQIA or not, resist the pressure to follow certain trends if you're secretly not that into them. If you're queer and can't get enough of tattoos and butch clobber, fill your Doc Marten boots and get tatted up to your heart's content. But if that doesn't do it for you, it in no way invalidates your identity. Equally, if you're straight and cis, you should still feel free to explore whatever style you want, whether it's 'traditional' for your gender or not. Care less about what other people think of your clothes and more about how your clothes make you feel.
4. Clothes have no gender.
5. Neither do hairstyles.
6. No matter what your sexuality is, you don't have to dress for the male gaze. Dress for your own goddamn gaze. And if you do want to use style for seduction, remember, whatever you're wearing, there's nothing sexier than confidence.
7. Any A-list actress, queer or otherwise, who dons a tailored tux on the red carpet will instantly be inundated with declarations of love from an army of sapphic superfans.

8. If you're searching for style inspiration, look to extraordinary fashion icons, both straight and queer. My personal muses are mostly dead movie stars and drag queens who overuse highlighter and innuendo as much as I do.

9. If, quite frankly, you don't give two hoots about fashion, that's totally cool too. Lean into comfort and practicality. Slip on some lovely, reliable, sensible shoes and channel your energies into whatever does float your boat.

10. When wielded with intention and creativity, style can be a powerful tool for self-expression and lorryloads of fun. If this rings true for you, then have at it. Spark your own joy by adorning yourself with garments that lift your spirits, reflect your unique identity and make you feel unstoppable. And by the way, from one lover of style to another, you look awesome.

CHAPTER 11

What happens when my heart breaks

London, 2014

She does not like how close I am with my female friends.

To be clear, I am not one of those lesbians who has secret crushes on my mates. My friends are mostly straight and, though I find them to be magnificent, I do not fancy them and they do not fancy me. But despite how many times I've re-assured Robyn of that, she is, I believe, jealous of the intimacy of these friendships. She does not like how affectionate I am with my friends, that I cuddle them if they need comforting or just because I'm so happy to see them I literally can't help it.

When I am with my friends, when she is not there, I feel like the truest version of me.

Here I am with Lela on one of our many outings. This time it's a burlesque ball she correctly deduced would be right up our alley. Naturally we're dolled up to the nines for this (and let's be honest, any) occasion. I'm in a crimson pencil dress, she's a vision in emerald satin. Our impromptu photo shoot starts off very forties film noir and rapidly descends into rambunctious tomfoolery, inexplicably using a giant pumpkin as a prop. Giddy and girlish, we sip cocktails from antique teacups, whoop at the dazzling performers and dance with abandon.

But our friendship isn't just about us both being glitzy goodtime girls. We have in-depth heart-to-hearts too. We are having one right now. We talk about the fun stuff, sure: the complex psychology of Marilyn Monroe, our favourite episodes of *Sex and The City*, the latest collections at Milan Fashion Week, which we can in no way afford but find so thrilling. But we talk about the tough, meaty stuff too: career struggles, family issues, relationship dilemmas. We speak for hours with absolute candour and compassion, dissecting our life problems in forensic detail, reminding each other of what we have been through, how far we have come and how strong we are.

I adore my friends and the fact that they adore me makes me value myself more. They are women I have found in my life who are creative, caring, passionate, non-judgemental, funny, wild and liberated. These are all qualities I hope I possess too, and when I'm with them, they see all that in me and it makes me see it in myself.

It's a piping hot day, I'm sunbathing in the park and I am with my girls. There's Shari, incredibly supportive, impeccably stylish and in possession of possibly the world's most infectious giggle. And Jess – a free spirit through and through, theatrical and adventurous – to name just two of these life-affirming women, or to use our collective noun and WhatsApp group chat name, Goddesses. We gossip and giggle and work on our tans. I'm soaking in the sunshine and the splendour of their company. Now Shari is teaching us how to power pose. She urges us all to do this next time we need to feel like a boss at work. We join in, leaping to our feet and placing our hands on our hips, a squad of invincible Wonder Women.

My friendships are fortifying and uplifting. Who I am with my friends is who I want to be in life. With them, I feel warm, open, thoughtful, vivacious and like I am full of infinite potential. My close female friendships are some of my most nourishing, long-lasting love stories.

But I have noticed something.

I have noticed that who I am with my friends is not who I am with Robyn. I have noticed that so many of the things my friends cherish about me are the very things I subdue when she is there. They are also some of my favourite things about myself: the flowing compassion, the unselfconscious exuberance, the raucous jokes, the joyful self-expression. But with Robyn I dial all that down, especially if we are in public together. I worry that uncensored me is not appealing enough in her eyes, so I am this other version of myself. It's not that I'm not being me, but I'm not being my whole self. I am shrinking parts of me to try and please her.

One night I am out with Robyn, on the dancefloor, having the time of my life. I love dancing. Always have done. Dancing makes me feel alive. And that's how I feel tonight on the dancefloor in this fabulous gay bar surrounded by my community. How awesome is this? I feel connected to myself. I am floaty and free.

Robyn pulls me to one side.

'Why are you dancing like that?'

'What do you mean? This is how I dance.'

'It's like you think you're in a music video. It's OTT.'

'I'm just having fun. What's the problem?'

'You'll give people the wrong idea. They'll think you're doing it for them.'

'I'm not doing it for them. I'm doing it for me.'

We return to the dancefloor, but my shine is dimmed.

I can't get back into the music. I feel embarrassed and self-conscious, but also nettled and confused. Why doesn't she like my dancing? Shouldn't she just be pleased I'm having a good time? When Justin Timberlake plays in the club and she busts out her most swaggering moves, I think, 'Yes, Robyn! Look at you go!' Why is it different for her?

From this night on, whenever I dance when Robyn is there, I hold a part of myself – my wildest, freest, most authentic part – back.

My friends love the way I dance and they dance with gusto themselves. I love to dance, but I do not dance like me any more, not when I'm with Robyn.

She is naturally dominant and in this relationship I become more submissive than I want to be. I was a different person when I fell for her. I was younger, greener and so ready to give everything it took to nurture this astonishing torrent of passion between us. Robyn has this unbridled, force-of-nature character that I find so attractive, but she is also more prone to confrontation than I am. I do not like conflict in relationships and to avoid conflict in this one I have to deny parts of myself.

One night we are out in a crowded bar with sticky carpets. We're both drinking, but Robyn's more drunk. I am only sipping my wine because I'm on edge. On nights like this my every move is under the microscope. When I'm not looking directly at her, I make a conscious effort to look down. I'm extremely careful not to talk to anyone or absentmindedly glance around the room, in case she mistakenly thinks I'm flirting. I cannot bear another round of baseless accusations. Despite my best efforts, another round of baseless accusations comes. She says it's because she's scared of losing me. She tells me that she worries I'm too good for her, as if the jealousy is a compliment. I wonder what my friends would think if they could see how I'm behaving now. Later, when I tell them about it, they will be concerned.

I also worry that those times I get upset, get overcome with feeling and let out all those feelings honestly without holding back, she seems faintly disgusted by such emotional outpouring. My friends do not react like this if I ugly-cry once in a while. My friends are not repulsed by the fullness of my emotions.

When I met Robyn, I was so excited to finally find this person, this funny, sexy lesbian who wanted to really be with me after all that time I'd been languishing in the closet. I fell so hard so fast. I was all in from the off, my heart served up on a plate. I was willing to blow up my life to be with her, to come out to my family, to move to the other side of the planet, to be whatever she wanted me to be. This relationship was the thing and I craved it so deeply, I was willing to sacrifice parts of myself at the altar of Us

I admit I tend to over-romanticize things. Maybe it's because I've always been a bookworm and a writer and a hopeless sap who can well up at an advert for cat food. From the beginning with Robyn, I immediately think of our relationship in extreme terms. I refer to it as 'the first big love of my life' and consider myself a 'Wuthering Heights romantic', because like Cathy and Heathcliff, I hail from Yorkshire and have a lot of feelings. Later on, I will realize that all-consuming Wuthering Heights-style love isn't exactly the healthiest thing to aim for, that it can in fact be quite toxic, but when I'm right there in the thick of it, it is epic and enthralling. The emotional intensity makes it feel like my life is suddenly full of meaning. But idealizing my relationship in this way, revering it to this extent, makes it so much harder to let go. The stakes feel so high. I have put so much on the line for this.

The relationship with Robyn is by no means all bad things. There are so many wonderful things, enough wonderful things to keep me there for six years. There is tenderness and togetherness and connection and love. So much love. But I know, when I speak honestly to myself or to my most trusted confidantes, that I am letting this relationship hold me back. To an extent, I am hiding in it and that's on me. I'm not throwing myself into pursuing my creative career ambitions because I have thrown myself so fully into this relationship, and because I secretly fear that the kind of woman who puts herself out there, who is an entertainer and a storyteller and a suck-all-the-marrow-out-of-lifer, is not a woman who would be lovable to Robyn. I have, in a sense, put my life on pause for six years. This is not her fault. I do not blame her for this. I was complicit in it all. I did it willingly. But I did it to try and ensure that I remained as loveable as possible in her eyes. I realize now that although Robyn and I care so much for each other, the truth is that fundamentally, we are incompatible. Something in her stifles a core part of me, makes me feel inhibited, self-conscious, ashamed.

These things I am dimming are all to do with creativity, communication and self-expression. They are things that feel so vital to who I believe myself to be, who I want to be in my life and career. In subduing them, I fear I am subduing myself.

After six years of doing it, I am exhausted. But then it hasn't really just been six years, has it? I have been doing this people-pleasing thing since childhood. I have spent all my years on Earth suppressing different parts of who I am to make others more comfortable, to make them like me more. It's why I stayed in the closet so long. And now I am finally out and in this lesbian relationship I wanted so much, and I'm still doing it. Squashing yourself down for so long chisels away at you.

Sometimes I worry about how much of myself, of my own original power and joy and lifeforce, I am eroding. If I keep on like this, how much of me will be left?

❋

So, it's 4 a.m., it's been six years and we haven't yet slept tonight. We have been lying here awake, in our double bed in our small room in a shared house in East London. We have been holding each other and talking and crying all night. There has been so much crying. The air is heavy with our sorrow.

Yesterday I ended things with Robyn. Tomorrow is my twenty-eighth birthday. In two weeks, it would have been our six-year anniversary. I have not fallen out of love with her. I have not met someone else. My heart is still bound up with hers. I still look at her and feel overcome with emotion. I still yearn for her to hold me. My instinct is still to run into her arms. Yet I have just broken both our hearts.

But I still have who I am with my friends and I really like that person. That feels like me at my best. It is the chasm between how I am with them and how I am with her that made me realize something is deeply wrong. It is the contrast between how they respond to my more creative, expressive, emotional sides and how she does, that underlines this revelation. My friends are my compass reminding me who I am when she is not there and who I was before I ever met her. My friends are the ones who guide me back to myself.

So here I am with Robyn in the aftermath of the self-inflicted devastation. I want so much to take it all back, to say, 'Forget it, babes. Let's keep trying to make it work. I am yours. Hold me, hold me, hold me.' I have to use every ounce of willpower I can muster to stop those words slipping out of my lips. I know this must end. However much I adore her, I have to hold onto myself now. This has gone on long enough. It is time to set us both free.

The one thing that is keeping me strong is the thought of me as a little girl and me as an old lady. I mentally zoom out from this moment in time and I see the entirety of my life, what has been and what is yet to come, as one big picture. I think of little girl me, a people-pleaser from the off, forever feeling I wasn't good enough, always so desperate to be deemed lovable, hiding the parts of myself I worried would make me less lovable, feeling excruciatingly ashamed of those parts, trying so hard to secure that soothing sunshine of another person's love.

I think of teenage me, staying in the closet all that time to keep myself lovable, still hiding, still trying so hard, still bending myself into unnatural shapes to be palatable, to be accepted, to be loved. And I think of me now in my late twenties. I am still doing it as an adult. I have come out of the closet, but I am continuing to diminish myself to try and keep hold of this lesbian love I miraculously found and am so terrified to lose.

I have been doing this people-pleasing, self-squashing routine for almost three decades. And then I think of old lady me in the future and I know that I do not want that to be the sum-total of her life. I do not want her to still be doing this exhausting, self-eroding, desperate, people-pleasing thing. I want her to look back on her life and know that she was as true to herself as she knew how to be. It is old lady me that keeps me firm in my resolve in this moment. I feel protective of her, just as I feel protective of little girl me who was always trying too hard to make other people happy. I don't want to be a watered-down version of myself any more. I cannot reach my deathbed only to look back on my life and know that it has been half-lived. I can't do that to her. I can't do that to me.

I know people-pleasing isn't something only gay women do, but I also know that as a woman I have been conditioned to put other people's comfort before my own and make myself as palatable as I can. And I know that as a gay person I have been taught, literally taught in school, to feel ashamed about my identity and keep it hidden to be accepted.

There is no hierarchy of heartbreak. I'm not trying to say my lesbian heartbreak hurts more than a straight person's heartbreak. It is all agony. But there is a particular pain within my lesbian heartbreak that is specific to it being sapphic. This relationship that is now over was the thing that, for me, made all the awful parts of being gay worth it. There was so much riding on this. This was the space where I got to finally have the connection I craved so much that I was willing to go against societal expectations and my parents' wishes to pursue it. And now it's over. The cocoon of our relationship is cracked wide open. Now I am left with the wreckage and all the people I have disappointed.

They say have no regrets, but I am full of them. I regret staying in this relationship for so long. I regret putting up with certain behaviour. I regret shrinking myself to try and make her happy. But I don't regret falling in love with her. How can I? It was a beautiful, agonizing, blissful, complicated, all-consuming, heady, humdrum, devastating, delicious experience. And when we were good, we were glorious.

I wonder if I have squandered my youth. If I have, then there it is. That is done. But at least I know myself better now. I know my boundaries. I know my worth. I know who I am and who I want to be. And I will move forward, however much it hurts.

Public places I weep in in the aftermath of my break-up

My desk at work.

Toilets at work.

Toilets at train stations.

Toilets at shopping centres (basically, anywhere there's a bog, there's a blubfest).

In the queue at Pret (she loved coffee).

In a heap on the floor of the self-help aisle in Waterstones, clutching a book called *Women Who Love Too Much*. (It happened one time, ok!)

On the tube, listening to a Spotify playlist called Sad. 'Wrecking Ball' by Miley Cyrus bursts into my eardrums. I know what's coming. I don't stand a chance. Tears fill my eyes before cascading down my face. I try to downplay this by angling myself away from the other passengers. But it's rush hour and the carriage is rammed, so I end up staring directly into a stranger's armpit, sobbing on the Central Line. Nobody looks up.

CHAPTER 12

Suddenly single

Peering out through the eyeholes of my papier-mâché mask at a room full of primary school children while trying not to sob is, admittedly, a new low.

It's the day after the break-up. I have barely slept and the only place I want to be is held in Robyn's arms. Alas, that is not an option because my idiotic, pre-break-up self agreed to take part in a children's theatre performance. My heart is full of pain and my head is full of thoughts.

Just look at all their happy little faces. Look at the hope in their eyes. Enjoy it while you can, kids. Won't be long before life comes along and destroys your dreams. You probably believe in fairytales. To be fair, I am encouraging that by acting one out for you right now, but lemme tell you, kids, life is not a fairytale! At least not for this rapidly-approaching-thirty, heartbroken lesbian . . .

I wonder what mine and Robyn's children would have looked like . . .

Ah, just when I thought I couldn't get any lower, I've found a new way to torture myself. Better sit with that thought for a while. Oh shit, it's me. What is my line?

. . . What is my life?

❉

When it comes to work, I'm flailing. My career is nowhere near where I want it to be. I've always loved writing. English and Drama were my best subjects at school. I edited my college magazine and wrote for my university paper. It all seemed like it might be building up to something, leading somewhere exciting, but then it didn't. I'd love to make a living by being creative but I have no master plan, useful contacts or financial safety net to make that happen. So instead, I am hurtling through my twenties at alarming speed, feeling like it's already too late to make something of myself.

Here I am sitting at the reception desk of the job I loathe that makes me loathe myself. A man in a dark suit strides in. He looks down his nose at me. To get a better view down my top. I smile tightly, take his name, offer him a beverage, arrange biscuits neatly on a plate for him, all the while seething with rage, at him, at these Hobnobs, at the mess I've made of my life. Back at my desk I surreptitiously scroll job boards, wishing I was anywhere but here.

Nevertheless, I'm trying. I do bits of journalism work experience and a lot of writing for free. I start a blog, get the odd freelance copywriting commission and apply for entry-level writing jobs that I never hear back from. Sometimes I get involved with stuff like this kids' theatre thing. I'm trying to do expressive things, trying not to let that side of me wither away completely, but it is all dispiritingly amateur. The media industry seems utterly impenetrable and those lists of extremely successful people under thirty make me feel even worse. I was an overachiever at school, yet I feel like an underachiever in life. I can't seem to translate my academic accomplishments into real world success. Glumly, I suspect I may have peaked aged eighteen.

Making a living through writing feels like an impossible fantasy and I have very real bills to pay. Ergo the miserable day job. And so I cling to any whisper of creativity I can, hoping that I will eventually figure it out and find my way. That is why I am currently wearing this papier-mâché mask and struggling not to cry in front of kids.

There are some days when my life feels like a tragic lesbian break-up montage. My feelings are dangerously close to the surface. I just feel so damn tender. It's like my whole being is one giant bruise and the slightest trigger presses directly onto my pain point. Cue the tidal wave of tears.

The incessant bawling is happening at home too. Due to offensively high London rents, Robyn and I have to keep living together in our one tiny room after we have split up. We are effectively holding a six-week vigil for our relationship, a week for every year we were together. It is intense. The atmosphere is always thick with something: sorrow, fear, doubt, nostalgia, desire, potential or a confusing mix of all of the above. Some days we give each other counsel and comfort. Other days we are stiff and stilted. We're beginning to withdraw and there is this new, strange distance growing between us.

Today is one of those distant days. I've been out with my friends and return home in an upbeat mood, which I try to play down so as not to offend Robyn. The result is that I'm speaking to her in an oddly formal way. As our room is so tiny and we avoid the communal lounge, we are trapped here together in this confined space with nowhere to sit except next to each other on the same bed. So we sit there, awkwardly. I pretend to be writing on my laptop, but get nothing done. She fiddles with her phone. But as the evening goes on, even though our brains know we aren't a couple any more, our bodies forget. Almost of their own accord, our bodies find each other and the physical proximity makes all the awkwardness melt away for a moment. I am filled instead with bittersweet pleasure at the feel of her skin against mine. When we make love, it is exquisite and tender and so, so sad. I am still in love with this woman.

In this period where we live together in one room but are no longer together as a couple, two contradictory things are occurring at once. We are drinking in every last drop of our intimacy, banking up as many memories and storing away as much closeness as we possibly can to sustain us through the winter ahead. But we are also, privately, on our own, figuring out the future and putting practical measures in place for our new lives as separate individuals. The date she is due to move back up North and I am due to move out looms large.

I have spent the vast majority of my twenties in relationships. Now, for the first time in almost a decade, I am both single and out of the closet. This is thrilling and terrifying. There is no new love on the horizon and if there was, I wouldn't want it. A big, questing part of me is eager to be on my own. To find out who I am when I'm not spending all my time with another person. Who am I when I'm not with her? Well, initially, a bit of a mess.

❈

I'm also struggling with logistics. I need somewhere to rent. My dream is to live alone. It feels important that in this defining new era of self-discovery I create a space that is just for me. But I don't have a lot of cash and London is not a city that embraces that quality in a prospective tenant. It turns out the streets of London are not paved with gold after all; they are paved with unaffordable, unappealing, poky little rooms in grimy house shares that are still, maddeningly, oversubscribed.

I scour Rightmove, Zoopla and Gumtree for studio flats that do not suck and ask everyone I know for leads. Most of the properties I view are mould-ridden shitholes that give me the heebie-jeebies. Or they just kind of . . . make no sense. Like, the bed will be wedged into a broom cupboard masquerading as a room – oh, and it's also rubbing noses with the oven. That doesn't seem like a fire risk at all! Or there are no windows, creating a sinister prison-cell effect. Or the shower is randomly slap bang in the centre of the living room. Worse, I find myself seriously contemplating, could I live somewhere I have to shower in the living room? I mean, if I'm living alone maybe it's . . . fine? If I have someone over, I could always tell them it's an art installation.

Morale low and skin itchy from all the fleapits I've been frequenting, I go to view a bedsit on the edge of suburbia. It's listed on the estate agent's website as a studio flat but, I realize as soon as I walk in, it has clearly had a former life as the modest front room of a family home. The 'kitchen' is three feet wide and perilously close to the bed. There is a tiny cubicle of a bathroom containing no bath, only a shower which practically hangs over the toilet and the sink is dollhouse tiny. I try it out for size and find I can only fit one of my human-sized hands in it at a time. On the plus side, what a timesaver! You can go to the lav, brush your teeth and shave your legs all at once, while making breakfast. There's also a fold-up bed that doubles as a 'convenient' desk, as long as you can be bothered to do the very inconvenient task of packing away all your bedding every morning. I ask how much the flat costs. The rent is £550 per month including bills. Ok, I can just about stretch to this. Although it may be comically cramped with multiple practical problems, it's infinitely better than anything else I've seen and I really don't want to deal with housemates as well as a broken heart. I snap the fucker up.

So now I am living on my own for the first time in my life. Yes, it's basically a bedroom with a hot plate and I can't even use said hot plate because every time I try it trips the electrics.

But the upside is that wherever I am in the flat, I can get to anywhere else in the flat with a maximum of five strides. I know that when I'm describing it now I'm emphasizing the flaws, of which there are many, but honestly? I bloody love my flawed little flat. It is the best place I have ever lived because it is all mine. Not literally. I am obviously renting. But that is how it feels. I have claimed this five-metre-squared space as my own. No matter what kind of shitshow of a day I've had, no matter how emotionally unstable I'm feeling, every single time I walk through that door and shut it behind me I look around at this perfectly imperfect sanctuary and breathe an audible sigh of relief. Finally, I am in my own space, in a home that I have made entirely for myself, and I adore it.

After years of sharing a living space with a partner with a very different style to me (she was strictly modern minimalism, I'm romantic, vintage maximalism), I relish the joy of decorating my new pad. I embark on a mission to transform it into a glamorously cosy, femme-fabulous retreat just for me. I put up black and white photos of my favourite Old Hollywood starlets, drape fringed shawls over the unsightly stains and line up my collection of sparkly shoes with glee. I own no furniture, as up until now I've always been in furnished accommodation. My new flat has the slightly scary fold-up bed and the unswitchonable hotplate but that's it, so I treat myself to a moving-in gift. There isn't room for a proper sofa but that doesn't bother me, because I have fallen in love with an antique chaise longue. It is petite, unabashedly girly, covered in tiny pink flowers and I'm obsessed with it.

With so much more free time on my hands, I decoupage a Billy bookcase from IKEA. I find a shocking pink, flat-pack chest of drawers online. It's the kind of garish home style choice you can only really get away with if you live alone. Ok, so it's technically meant to be furniture for a little girl, but it would be wasted on a little girl. She'd probably scribble all over it and pee in the drawers. I'll only do that when I'm wankered. I construct it myself, *The Blue Planet* documentary playing on my laptop as it's the only thing I can think of that's epic enough to score this moment. David Attenborough's rich, reassuring voice keeps me calm as I attempt to assemble my gorgeous monstrosity. It feels so symbolic, so powerful, so indicative of what an independent, grown-up woman I now am, me building my pink little girl's drawers.

Hours later, I am still slumped on the floor, surrounded by debris, wrestling my home into existence. When I've finally finished labouring and I'm sweating buckets, I behold my masterpiece. I have made . . . a dollhouse? A miniature pink replica whale? No, I have made a mess, just an absolute mess of my flat. But I have also made a whole set of drawers. I'm not totally confident I'll be able to put anything inside them or the structure may well collapse, but still, I'm out here doing this thing! This is empowerment, through DIY.

The drawers feel like a major win, but I am still emotionally wobbly. Like many sapphics, I have a tendency to go all-in on feeling my feelings. My two contrasting emotional states (optimism vs. despair – who will win today?!) are scored by and expressed through the music I'm listening to – alternately upbeat, empowering 'go get 'em, lady-tiger' anthems, and bleak heartbreak melodies. I confess I do listen to James Blunt's 'Goodbye My Lover' more times than one person probably should. On the down days, there are *a lot* of tragic sapphic tracks to choose from too. There's a whole subgenre of music we could just label 'sad lesbian songs', from k.d. lang with her 'Constant Craving' to Tracy Chapman's 'The Promise'. As a community, we have most definitely made pining into an artform.

The question on deck is: how do I get over my ex when

I'm still in love with her? I plough my energy into carving out my own space, not just literally by making my humble flat feel like home, but also in my wider life. I have, to some extent, been voluntarily suppressing my whole self for years and now I want to reclaim that territory. I crave self-discovery, creativity and a sense that I am living on a bigger, braver scale. For so long, my relationship was the thing. So, I wonder, what is the thing now?

I am faced with a kind of queer existential crisis. Up until now, the whole point of me being queer was to be queer with her. For six years, my sexuality was defined by my lesbian relationship. That was the physical manifestation of my lesbianism and, in truth, my favourite thing about being gay. She was the reason I went through the rigmarole of coming out. When people didn't believe someone as feminine as me could be a homosexual, she was the living proof I provided to shut them down. She was my chosen family. Her gay friends became my gay friends. She was the one who introduced me to so much queer culture, from lesbian parties to sapphic cinema. She was my gateway to the community. And now she is gone. I am left with the fragments of a failed relationship and broken-glass bits of queerness that used to be bound together by my connection to her. How do I affirm my identity now I'm sapphic-ing solo? How do you exist as a queer person when your queer relationship ends?

Like being queer, being single by choice means consciously rejecting the pressure to conform to a traditional relationship. It means going against the grain and inhabiting an identity that is othered by society and often made to feel lesser than. The state of singledom among women is painted as something tragic. The implication is that a single woman has failed. She has failed at holding down a relationship. She has failed at securing a spouse. If she is gay, she has also failed at being straight. So now she must be condemned to a life of public humiliation, private loneliness and frequent heartfelt lip-synching to Celine Dion power ballads while somehow simultaneously blubbing into a tub of Ben & Jerry's in the manner of Bridget Jones.

I'm not saying that my single years do not include a great deal of this kind of caper. I can be klutzy and say the embarrassing thing because I panic in awkward silences and regularly swing between overindulgence and determined self-restriction. Make no mistake, I can do a very convincing impression of a lesbian Bridget Jones. But that is not the whole story. The emotional truth of being single is not just one thing. It is not a stereotype.

Finally having my own place gives me the space and privacy I need to grieve our relationship properly. On my own, I go over everything with a fine-tooth comb and process both where I went wrong and why I stayed for so long. Slowly, I start to get some distance from it all.

Like grief, the process of mourning the relationship is neither straightforward nor linear. Sometimes I feel exhilarated about embarking on new adventures. Other times, especially at night, I am struck with an all-consuming loneliness, wondering if I will be on my own for eternity. I weep with futile yearning, pawing at the void next to me where a person, *my person*, used to be beside me. There are times when I'm so low, all I can do is close my eyes and picture us in those early days full of passion and promise. I feel deep sadness at the distance between how we were at our best and how we are now. I physically ache for our lost tenderness.

In my weaker moments when it all gets too much, I wonder if expressing my whole self is all it's cracked up to be. There are times when, honestly? I would give all of myself over to her once more, just for the comfort of being back in her arms.

Alone in bed, I spoon my pillow and pretend it's her. You can't get your heart broken cuddling up to a cushion. Unless you accidentally look in a mirror. Then it's game over.

Despite how tough it can be, in time I find I actually love being single. Apart from those times when I do not love it at all. I find solace in knowing I have done the right, brave thing by leaving a relationship that was not right and did not make me brave. And after a thorough cathartic weeping session, I find I can mostly bounce back from these dips. I discover that I am more resilient than I knew. I also find that those friendships I have formed with Lela, Shari, Jess and all the other incredible women in my life, make me stronger. They fortify and nourish me in a profound way. I learn that I don't have to be in a romantic relationship to be happy after all. As it turns out, my single years contain some of the happiest, horniest and more empowering times of my life.

❊

Now I'm single I have loads more free time to spend with my mates. Tonight, we are out at a pop-up prohibition party. We have all dressed up for the occasion. I am living for this 1920s theme, in a strappy silver vintage dress, pearls that dangle to my waist, a faux fur stole and a diamante necklace repurposed as a headband. I have tucked my long hair under itself and secured it with dozens of kirby grips to create a makeshift flapper bob. Not going to lie about it, I'm loving this look. I'm also loving wearing something so unashamedly glamorous. My friends look spectacular in their finery too. We have pre-drinks and arrive at the secret location, a ballroom in the centre of town, giddy and fizzing with anticipation.

We burst into the room and this is just incredible. The wildest, most decadent party of my Great Gatsby dreams. A live band is onstage playing up-tempo, old-timey music.

Burlesque dancers are moving through the crowd, twirling giant feather fans above their heads. People are carrying placards saying things like 'END PROHIBITION NOW' and 'WE WANT LIQUOR!' Everyone looks amazing, all dressed up with somewhere fabulous to go. We grin manically at each other, pointing out every new exquisite detail we notice, so we can all gasp in delight at this jaw-dropping shindig.

We grab cocktails from the bar and they all have darling names: French 75, Tom Collins, Bees Knees. Already, I am having so much fun. My shoulders start to twitch in time with the beat. We down our drinks and head for the dancefloor. I start to dance, then I catch myself. It's a reflex. I am so used to holding back when I'm dancing, keeping an eye on how expressive I am, trying not to be too much. I've been doing it for years. And then at this 1920s party surrounded by my gorgeous, goodtime girls, I realize the glorious truth. I can dance like myself again.

I throw my whole body, my whole being, into the music. I improvise a Charleston, shimmying my hips and flinging my arms and kicking my legs up. I have the biggest smile on my face. I look around at my friends and see that they do too. I feel so liberated and so pure and so connected to these magnificent women. We dance and we laugh and we hug each other all night long. They tell me how much they love me, how proud they are of me, and I tell them the same. It is exactly the platonic love-in I need. We are uninhibited and having the time of our lives. We are wild and together and free.

Things I love about being single

More time for my friends.

More time for myself.

More time for real, meaningful self-reflection.

Making my home my own, which means making it as pink as possible.

Rewatching my favourite trashy reality TV shows for the umpteenth time without judgement.

Never having to send a check-in text when I'm on a night out and enjoying the moment.

Playing my favourite cheesy music *really* loud.

Bedroom dance parties for one.

Using the other half of my double bed for storage.

Nobody I have to hide my drunk online shopping purchases from.

Flirting (tentatively at first, rustily, but nevertheless thrillingly).

Possibility.

CHAPTER 13

I love women's bodies, but can I love my own?

In the aftermath of my break-up, I am so in bits I stop eating and start drinking. Heavily. Solids barely pass my lips. The thing I have been hoping for since childhood finally happens! It's a miracle; my appetite has evaporated. The weight drops off. I'm suddenly the skinniest I've ever been. People notice my rapid metamorphosis. They say things like, 'Oh my god, you look . . . amazing. What's your secret?' Losing the love of my life, you insensitive fucker. You want to know the secret? The secret is my heart is broken. As is my cooker. Regret for breakfast, shame for lunch, skipped dinner to make a playlist called Songs To Cry To. But also, ohmygod-icantbelievehowslimiam. Hello, collarbones, so nice to finally meet you!

I realize that being obsessed with thinness is neither endearing nor feminist. But it is a strange, and undeniably intoxicating, experience to suddenly lose a bunch of weight by accident, as someone who has been trying desperately to lose weight since primary school. As a child, I was routinely teased for my size, given cruel nicknames by classmates and subjected to stinging comments from family members. From an early age I was extremely concerned about the protrusion of my tummy and the circumference of my thighs.

I remember when I was eight years old. I was at a friend's house with three other girls. One girl had a bright idea for a super fun game. We should all take turns to weigh ourselves in front of each other and then compare and contrast the results. I did not need to step on the scales to know that I was by far the biggest, that I had lost this horrifying contest before it even started. I did not want to play. This ordeal sounded like a waking nightmare, a communal ceremony to ensure my public humiliation. But if I protested that would only make my weight more of an issue, draw everyone's attention to it, and, most appallingly of all, invite their comments about my body even more. So I kept my anxiety quiet and the game went ahead. We each took turns to step onto the scales and our weight was announced to the group. In news that came as a shock to nobody, the girl who suggested this game was the lightest. I was, of course, the heaviest. I burned with shame. When I went home later that day, I refused to eat. I looked at my too-big body in the mirror and I hated every inch of it with the sort of aggressive, nasty loathing that women only ever reserve for themselves.

As a teenager, my obsession with slimming grips me even tighter. I start doing my mum's Lizzie Webb home workout tape from the 1980s every morning before school. I fall into a pattern that will plague me for decades: eating nothing at all for several days and then, ravenous and reckless, suddenly abandoning my starvation diet and gorging on half a loaf's worth of hot, buttery toast.

During my adolescence, just as our culture is filled with negative representation of queer people, it is filled with negative representation of women who aren't thin. The nineties and noughties are a particularly bad time for women. I mean, you could look at almost the whole of history and describe it as 'a particularly bad time for women', but the reason these two decades are especially toxic, one of the reasons anyway, is the way women's bodies are talked about and treated. Diet culture and the glorification of extreme thinness is omnipresent. Fatphobia, like homophobia, is rampant.

I come of age when size zero is all the rage. Weight-loss companies, bitchy relatives and gossip mags are all ramming their pesky diet culture down my throat when all I really want down my throat is something tasty and comforting. In *Heat* magazine I see the vicious 'circle of shame', added to paparazzi photos of female celebrities to scrutinize their cellulite and 'muffin tops'. I read articles about 'the lollipop look', a trend describing women who are so svelte their heads appear huge in comparison to their tiny bodies. God, I want to be a lollipop lady. I crave so desperately to be thin. I long to see my bones protruding through my skin. I stare in the mirror, hunch my shoulders forward to hollow out my clavicles and suck in my cheeks, wishing I could maintain this effect without having to hold my breath and contort my body so bizarrely.

To be overweight is to be a subject for ridicule and disdain. Cruel fat jokes are everywhere and deemed entirely socially acceptable. I see literally no plus size queer characters on-screen, except for Lea DeLaria playing the butch butt of the joke in the *Friends* episode, 'The One with The Lesbian Wedding'. When *The L Word* and its British counterpart *Lip Service* come along, I adore them both, but all the main queer characters in both shows are uniformly slim. I barely see anyone who looks like me in what little queer media there is, apart from the occasional 'thick and juicy' contestant on *RuPaul's Drag Race*.

So, like much of womankind, I've wasted an inordinate amount of time despairing over my appearance. When I look at my own body, flaws are all I see. I can do an inventory of everything I feel is wrong with it, from the top of my too-round head to the tip of my overly stubby toe. Too much like a blancmange, too many visible seams. This obsessive mental cataloguing of my physical flaws does not feel good. I have sobbed over photographs I didn't know were being taken where they've upchinned me without consent. I have also sobbed over photographs I posed for, my smile rictus in grim dread anticipating the inevitably mortifying end result. I have exercised to excess and injured myself. I can remember word for word every body-shaming comment that has ever been made to me since I was a little (although never little enough) girl. I struggle to remember the compliments or kindnesses. Why is it the painful words that stick?

I have cancelled outings at the last minute, because I was in such a self-hating fog I literally couldn't bear for anyone to witness me and my hideousness. I remember one time I was in my bedroom, getting ready for a party, but somehow every outfit I tried made me loathe my reflection more. I crumpled in a heap on the floor, a mess of a person in this mess of a room, surrounded by my discarded, treacherous clothes, and I wept in frustration and self-hatred. Unable to face the world, I made up an excuse, manufactured a pretend highly contagious virus, and locked myself away so I wouldn't have to endure the torment of anyone looking at me.

This war I am waging against myself has gone on since childhood and I know I'm not the only one. Intellectually, I can see this is not a good use of my time. There is work to be done, equality to be fought for, life-changing queer representation to be created. I wonder what I could have achieved if I hadn't spent quite so much time feeling terrible about my appearance. This body-hating routine is boring and self-obsessed, but it is also a really hard habit to break.

I've been at the mercy of the industrial diet complex for yonks. I've bought into the fads and yo-yoed like a brainwashed trooper. But none of these diets have ever been anywhere near as effective as the Smash Your Heart to Smithereens and Be So Broken You Can't Bring Yourself To Eat Plan I'm currently on.

When people marvel at how much weight I've lost and tell me I look great, they mean it as a compliment. Part of me – the diet culture-conditioned part, the insecure, self-loathing, serial-starver part – feels buoyed up, high on the praise and my lack of calories. They think I look good. I've lost the weight I've been trying to lose forever. I've finally succeeded at that ultimate feminine aspiration of being slim. But a significant, more lingering part of me feels nettled. If I look 'so much better' now, exactly how awful did they think I looked before? And why is it that everyone tells you that you look the best you've ever looked when you feel at your all-time lowest?

Some people assume that queer women are immune to all the body image bollocks, but from personal experience I know that to be a fallacy. After all, we still live in the same messed up world as the straights. It's hard enough being a person with a body in our society. But when you're queer, there's this whole other aspect to grapple with. People fundamentally object to the existence of our queer bodies. They object to what they look like, what they do, what they desire.

As if that wasn't enough to contend with, within Lesboland there is very much an unattainable beauty standard – namely effortless, androgynous swagger complete with washboard abs, sculpted jawlines and perky chests. I see this in lesbian TV heartthrob characters like Shane in *The L Word* and Frankie in *Lip Service*. When I come out, I don't feel lean or androgynous enough to qualify as a 'hot queer'. This narrow version of what's attractive can cause many of us to feel that we are not enough. For me, this sense that my body doesn't fit in my own community feels almost like a double betrayal.

I'm far from the only queer person who has battled body image demons. A 2019 survey commissioned by the Mental Health Foundation shows that LGBTQIA people are more likely to suffer with mental health issues related to body image. A third of queer people have experienced suicidal thoughts related to body image, compared to 11 per cent of heterosexual people. The statistics are even more alarming for bi folks. The tyranny of queer beauty standards isn't just an issue in the women's scene. Gay men can feel even more pressure to conform to an unattainably lean, muscular physique.

So how do we navigate our relationships with our bodies as LGBTQIA people? The body image conversation often excludes us, but we need to talk about it. How do we ultimately find peace and self-compassion in a world that not only tells us our bodies look wrong, but that what our bodies crave and do is wrong too? And, importantly, how do we harness our collective energy, stop using it to beat ourselves up and start using it to campaign for a world with equality for bodies of all sizes, sexualities, genders, races and abilities?

The world tells us to be straight. The world also tells us we should look a certain way to be worthy. Are we sensing a theme here? The world doesn't give a rat's ass about what's best for us. It just wants to put us in a box and keep us in our place. We are made to feel like it is our bodies that are the problem. We feel shame for how our bodies look and what our bodies want. I have felt that gnawing shame, that desperation to shrink and hide the sins and yearnings of my body. I have felt myself to be too much, too hungry, too perverse. Like homophobia, fatphobia is a means to keep us small, to contain us and make us turn in on ourselves. But it is society that is broken, not our bodies. It is society that teaches us to be ashamed of how we look and who we are. Society tells us:

be narrow. Be straight. Take up less space. Feel shit about yourself. Be ashamed.

It all comes back to shame, doesn't it? For so long I felt deep shame for my body, for its size and proportions, but also for what my body desired. I felt shame for its appetites, the way it craved both food and women. My body would not do what I willed it to do. It refused to be slim and it refused to be straight, this unruly, wayward body of mine. But even when I began to embrace my body's desire for women, I still struggled to embrace my body itself.

As I begin to heal from my break-up and start to eat again, the weight creeps back on and my body gradually returns to its usual state. But something else happens that transforms how I feel about it. When I start dating different women in my late twenties, the impact on how I feel about my body is life-changing. It is exciting and euphoric. I can't believe how good the sex is. Sometimes it is so good I have an urge to pause mid-move and call a friend to tell them about this incredible shag I'm having. I know they'd be happy for me! Not only is it an absolute treat to suddenly be having lots of lovely lady-orgasms, it is also healing.

The first time I sleep with a woman who has a body like mine, it is really quite something. She is hot, her body is hot. Sensual, soft, so different to the other more angular women I've slept with in the past. She is a sexy revelation. She helps me appreciate how desirable a body like mine could be.

I realize that there is a big difference in the way I look at my body and the way I look at the body of another woman I am in bed with. When I look at myself, I zoom in on what I hate. But when I gaze at a woman I am being intimate with, my eyes see so much to lust after. I am, without exception, mesmerized by the beauty of her body, whatever shape or size it is. I have been with women who are far leaner than me and those who wear a bigger dress size than I do. And I have fancied the pants off them all.

When I think honestly about the bodies I am attracted to, not the ones I am told are attractive but the ones I actually, authentically desire, I see that they are all different. I also see that I'm attracted to so much more than a woman's body. I am lit up by the glint in her eye, the way she makes me laugh uncontrollably, the timbre and cadence of her voice, how she moves through the world, her passion, her fire, her tenderness.

I start to wonder if being a lesbian could help me to finally accept my body. I've rejected the male gaze and now I am shedding patriarchal beauty standards with every sapphic thrust. Each guttural moan is an unadulterated fuck-you to the tyranny of heteronormativity and an enthusiastic fuck-me to the magnificence of queer desire.

Look, I realize desirability isn't the be all and end all, and it's not like sleeping with women has cured me of all my hang-ups. Embracing my sexuality has reframed how I think about myself, but it has not fixed every one of my body image demons. That battle is ongoing, but it's not quite as sharp and serrating as it used to be. I don't loathe myself with quite the same ferocity. Maybe that's partly growing older too, realizing what a colossal waste of your precious remaining time on Earth hating yourself with such fury really is.

I'm not saying the only way to love your body is to have loads of gay sex (although what a fun prescription that would be). What I am saying is that it can be liberating to open your mind to the possibility that all different kinds of bodies, including your kind of body, might just be divine.

We don't have to want what they tell us to want. We don't have to be who they urge us to be.

Diary of a serial dieter

Here are some of the diets I have tried, tested and abandoned.

Special K diet
Failed to drop a dress size, didn't feel Special. Not oK.

Chewing and spitting out your food diet
Not advisable on a date.

Cabbage soup diet
Just as farty as you'd imagine. Terrible for socializing and global-warming.

Baby food diet
No wonder they're always crying.

Potato diet
Mashed, boiled, baked – who knew tatties were so versatile? However, this diet did not make me feel any less like a potato.

Juice cleanse
Really made me miss the simple pleasure of mastication.

Wine and egg diet
Not as fun as it sounds. They ration your wine and you get terrible wind.

SlimFast
They should rename this one AngryFast.

Prosecco diet
Gained two pounds in a week. Was too pissed to care.

Fist diet
To be honest, I totally got the wrong end of the stick here. Turns out it's about portion control. I'd hoped it was going to be a lot more racy.

CHAPTER 14

Hello, Brenda!
The gay lady dating
scene and other magical,
soul-destroying things

There's a lesbian dating app called Brenda?! I learn this during an app-downloading frenzy in 2014, when I discover that while I've been coupled up, dating apps have undergone a major image makeover. Once they were deemed embarrassing and a bit desperate, but they have now become ubiquitous.

I do not want a partner. Not in a romantic, committed, potential-to-turn-into-something-long-term sense. I had one of those and it eclipsed everything else in my life. But I do crave chemistry. I could really use a fix of horny human connection. I am not looking for love, but I am longing for lust. I want to feel something, and someone, new. Really, I just want to find someone hot who thinks I'm hot too, so we can do hot stuff together. I don't feel bad about wanting sex. I feel neither shame nor embarrassment for being a woman with a sexual appetite. I'm at a point in my life where I can finally own my sexual self, not just my sexual orientation but myself as a sexual being. As long as everyone involved is safe and comfortable, I just honestly don't see anything wrong with consenting adults having a great time getting it on. In fact, I want to be one of them!

That is why I'm on Brenda. The girls are all over Brenda. They can't get enough of Brenda. Their selfies flood my phone screen. I am suddenly carrying a whole throng of queer women around with me in my mobile wherever I go. I also download Tinder and Her. I start swiping and scrolling with enthusiasm. Dating apps should be brilliant for queer people. They eliminate the need for gaydar. They connect a disparate group via the power of the internet and the homosexual horn. Well, that's the theory at least.

But I confess I am not thriving on the apps. I get matches, but nothing seems to really go anywhere. I don't know how to start conversations without sounding ridiculously lame or offputtingly eager. There's a lot of mediocre chit-chat and I'm terrible at keeping on top of all the DM admin. Messaging too often fizzles out into virtual tumbleweed. I quickly become weary of the monotony of exchanging lacklustre DMs with other disenchanted strangers. Alas, I find no potential lovers or even anyone to meet up with for a drink on a Thursday night.

The closest I come to an app date is when I match with a stunning woman called Katia on Tinder. We start chatting and she's replying more quickly than people usually do on here. We're really getting on. It's bubbly, fun and flirty. Shock, horror, I'm actually enjoying a dating app! The next evening I'm alone at home, messaging Katia. I look at her picture again. She really is gorgeous. Long raven locks and striking features and I could definitely be into her. I wonder about suggesting we take our frisson offline and actually venture out on a date in the real world. But before I do that, I look her up on social media.

Within five minutes of Facebook stalking, I have found her. She only has one photo and it's the same as her Tinder profile picture. She also only has one friend, a middle-aged, bald man.

I have nothing against bald men, but Katia really did have such lovely hair. I get a sick feeling in the pit of my stomach as I crack the most obvious case of mistaken identity this century. Yes folks, Katia is a catfish. A fake profile set up by some geezer to dupe unsuspecting app-users. I feel very silly and very naïve. I am also really disappointed that the magnificent Katia is a mirage. I start to understand why so many people say dating sucks.

Disappointed by these newfangled apps, I sign up to the old-school dating website gaydargirls.com. As I'm filling out my dating profile I'm asked to check a box to indicate if I am a top (giver), bottom (receiver) or versatile (ambisextrous). Feeling cavalier, I tick all three, thinking that way I'll get more matches. Over the next few weeks, I receive some very interesting messages indeed. None of the 'Hey, how's your day?' or even less imaginative 'Hey's on here. On Gaydargirls I may not always fancy the women messaging me, but I do always appreciate how intriguing their messages are, how niche, how gripping.

I receive a message from a nineteen-year-old who wants to call me 'Mummy' in bed. Some people might find this surprising, but I am not surprised by this. I recognize that in others' eyes I have long had a touch of the cougars about me. In school plays I was typecast as the sexually predatory middle-aged woman. Which is a bit of a backhanded compliment when you're twelve. Ever since then, I've been told that my celebrity lookalike is Nigella Lawson. I don't look anything like her at all. We just both have dark hair and big boobs. I've always taken it as a ridiculously over-generous compliment. She may be twenty-six years my senior, but Nigella is a goddess. So I get the cougar thing. Heck, I was being referred to as a cougar back when it was called a MILF. People always just sort of thought I had that 'randy mum' look. And I am not here to yuck anyone's yum, but I am also not interested in fulfilling this particular fantasy with this random person on the internet. But you know, it's nice to know I could if I wanted to.

A few days later I receive a message from another user, this time a butch woman wearing a fabulous second-hand trouser suit. In her opening line she volunteers her services as my 'vintage daddy' and, while I admire her dapper swagger, this is all getting a bit too Oedipal for my liking.

It's not all women wanting me to be their mummy or them to be my daddy. Some are even more forward than that. Bored at work one day, I surreptitiously log into my Gaydargirls account on my desktop. I am greeted by a notification that I have a new message. Ooh, fun! I open it up and my whole computer screen, my *work* computer screen, is filled with a very Not Safe For Work close-up photograph of a vulva. Now I had gathered, from popular culture and my straight and bi friends, that being a single woman can mean being subjected to a tsunami of unwanted dick pics. I had not heard of the lesser-sighted, unsolicited fanny flash. I am surprised, amused, unoffended but definitely not aroused. Don't get me wrong, I am a fan of vulvas broadly speaking, but I do find them a lot more enticing when you can actually see the person they're attached to. Call me a prude, but a disembodied minge does nothing for me. What is the thought process behind sending that message? Great that they have such healthy vag-esteem, but does this technique ever actually work, using their minky as their chat up line?

I suspect I might have better luck meeting women face to face, as opposed to face to fanny. So I start investigating London's queer scene as a single woman. On a night out at a cheesy gay bar with a queer guy friend, I notice a beautiful woman smiling at me. We get chatting, get grinding up against each other on the dancefloor and I go home with her. The impression I've been given by popular culture is that one-night stands are uniformly terrible – soulless, unsatisfying and awkward for all concerned. But this one is bloody fantastic. The morning after our explosive night before, I kiss her goodbye and saunter out of her flat with a pep in my step and a smug grin plastered all over my face. It's less walk of shame, more stride of pride. Hello world, I'm a goddamn rock star. This was exactly what I needed. We swapped bodily fluids, but not phone numbers. I am incandescent, glittering with post-coital power.

I discover I have much more luck finding someone to snog on the scene than I do online. On nights out, I'm worried no one will believe I'm gay, so I overcompensate by flirting in a very obvious, mildly drag-queen-dressed-up-as-Nigella way. When I spot someone I fancy, I tap into my arsenal of seduction techniques which I deploy, to be honest, really quite brazenly. I experiment with the art of suggestive eye contact – gazing at the person, then looking away coquettishly before glancing back and letting my eyes linger. I jut out my bosom and pout with intent. Ridiculous, I know, but undeniably effective. Yet despite all this OTT flirting like a wanton hussy from another era, the beginning of every conversation is still taken up with the other person interrogating me to ensure I am actually queer.

I am out at a lesbian hip-hop night in East London when I spot her. This incredible, tattooed woman with a shaved head and a spark in her eye. She is so fucking fit. A combination of stunning bone structure, flawless features and butch swagger. She looks like Poussey from *Orange Is the New Black*, who I happen to have a humungous crush on. I assume she is out of my league. I assume that I am nowhere near cool or attractive enough to appeal to someone so clearly in the premier league of aspirational queer hotness. She catches me looking at her and her devastating face breaks out into this big, cheeky grin.

I melt into a puddle. God, I fancy her. And from the way she's looking at me, holy fuck, I think she might feel the same. After a fair bit of checking each other out across the dancefloor, she moseys over and offers to buy me a drink. Bloody hell, this is happening.

I sip my cocktail and we talk and the eye-fucking intensifies. She flirtatiously tells me she's a stud. I'm not 100 per cent sure what this means, but I bet it will be a lot of fun finding out. She tells me her biggest turn-on is turning me on. A few drinks later, we're kissing and it's just as sensational as I knew it would be. I give her my number and head home feeling like I'm walking on air.

On our first date we go to a bar in Angel that she suggests. I look up and see the ceiling is clustered with dangling bras. Subtle. We don't go home together that night, but we do a week later and it really is extraordinary. For the following days, I float around on a multiple-orgasm-fuelled high. But I also have a worrying thought. Am I accidentally being extremely rude? Am I stealing all the orgasms from the orgasm buffet? I am experiencing my first flurry of PPG: Pillow Princess Guilt. Of course, I shouldn't feel guilty about getting off if this makes us both happy. And she sure seems like she's enjoying herself too. I tell myself that surrendering to the bliss is an act of feminist empowerment and the defiant reclamation of queer pleasure. Which is true, as well as being a great excuse for more horny hijinks. She does eventually let me take the reins and that's how I discover two essential principles of sapphic sexual science: labels aren't always for life and topping a top is hot.

Ours is a brief fling, but our passion burns brightly. I don't feel sad or all that surprised when she leaves my last message on read. I wasn't emotionally invested. I honestly just felt really chuffed to attend a party for two between the sheets with her for as long as I did. I was not distraught when the party ended, just happy I'd been invited. I notice that her WhatsApp profile picture has changed to a couple selfie with a beautiful woman. I wonder if that's the recent ex-girlfriend she mentioned and whether they're back together. If so, good for them. I will always look back fondly at our wild nights spent raiding the orgasm buffet and giving in to bliss.

✣

While I'm having some dating adventures and fun flings, I'm also discovering that finding new people to sleep with is time-consuming and there's no guarantee it will be great, so I do the inevitable. I message my ex. Not Robyn. I'm not going to reopen that door. There's too much real emotion there. And, as I have deduced from social media, she's already moved on with a brand-new girlfriend anyway.

I text Kiara. We haven't spoken in years, but she lives in London now too. Sex with an ex often gets a bad reputation, but I'll be honest, sex with this ex is pretty great. I already know the chemistry is good, but also that we don't work as a couple, so it doesn't feel too emotionally pressured. We only meet up the once. Any more might veer dangerously close to relationship territory. But I'm glad that we do. It is nice to be with someone who knows me that way. Of course, it also makes me think about Robyn. I am still thinking about her more than I would like to.

A few months later, just over a year after my big break-up, I am doing a bit of routine emotional self-harming and stalking her new girlfriend on Facebook. Then the post pops up. They are engaged. I am stunned. This feels fast. I'm not sure I'm ready for another girlfriend and she's just signed up for a wife. Wow. I campaigned for equal marriage and now I'm being punished.

I feel betrayed, even though I have no right to feel that way. After all, it was me who called time on our relationship. It's not just that she is moving on that hurts, but that she is moving on at what feels like lightning speed. It is making me reassess our whole relationship and re-examine my perception of it. All the grandiose things I tell myself about what we had – that it was this deep, abiding romance for the ages that will forever shape us and stay in our hearts – well, those things might not be so unshakably true after all.

Rationally, I understand we have ended. She has a new life and she wants love in it. Fair play. I would never deny her that. I genuinely do want her to be happy and fulfilled. I suppose my pride is ruffled. That must be at least part of what I'm feeling, the sting that I am not so hard to get over after all. In the end, she is probably doing me a favour by moving on. It gives me a jolt. It forces me to realize that we really are finished. I have been replaced, quite easily it seems, with someone new. It is, inevitably, making me feel more distant from Us. She has a new Us now, with this whole other woman. I am not hers and she is not mine. Not any more.

Opening messages I receive on dating apps

'I like to wrestle. I've got a lesbian wrestling club. Do you wrestle?'

'If you were a vegetable, what would you be and why?'

'Marry me?'

FANNY FLASH

'I have a lesbian roller derby team. Would you like to join? Are you balanced?'

'Sit on my face.'

'Do you want to be my next mistake?'

CLIT PIC

'Is it raining or are you just pleased to see me?'

'Why are you dressed like that in your photos? Are you in fancy dress?' (I wasn't.)

'Hi. Just to be upfront from the start as I have been burned before, do NOT message me if you are a timewaster, a cheater or have just split up with your ex. If none of these apply, happy to chat.'

SNATCH SELFIE

'Grab your water gun, because I'm gonna make you squirt.'

'You're quite hot.' (Quite?!)

'What song would be the soundtrack to your life? Mine is "Creep" by Radiohead.'

VULVA WITH A WINKY FACE EMOJI

CHAPTER 15

Yes, it counts!

Like all great epiphanies, it happens in a sex club. I'm with my gal pal, Bessie, on a short summer getaway to Berlin. It's her birthday and her birthday wish is to visit a den of iniquity. Bessie has read about this place online and her heart is set on a scandalous night of debauchery.

We're queuing up outside the venue, an innocuous concrete slab of a building covered in graffiti. Giddy in the balmy night air, we are buzzing from a cocktail of anticipation and trepidation, as well as the actual cocktails we just drank. We aren't sure if we'll get in, what with the city's famously strict door policies, but we're determined to give it our best shot.

Being sex club novices, we haven't got the memo about the standard sex club dress code: latex, lace, strategically placed cut-outs for your nips. Instead, we are wearing summery bar-hopping ensembles. Bessie is in a cute top and jeans. I'm in a polka dot mid-century sundress and peeptoe wedges. Wedges! At a sex club! What am I thinking?? We look perfectly lovely, but not exactly the kink scene's wet dream. At the front gate, a bouncer in leather chaps gives us a cursory glance. We await his verdict with bated breath. He shakes his head, distinctly unimpressed and unconvinced.

A man of few words and two visible buttocks, he declares, '*Nein*.'

Bessie's sexually liberated face falls. Oh crap. I really do want her to have the best birthday ever and this is her one birthday wish. She's been such a good friend to me and I totally adore her. The least I can do is give her a lovely birthday knees-up (and whatever else goes up in these gaffs). I snap into action. I need to sort this out and get this little lady in this sex club sharpish. Doesn't Assless Chaps understand? *Hello, it's her birthday*. He's obviously not au fait with the international rules of birthdays. You don't say no to a sweet angel of a girl on her birthday. That's just mean and also, really missing the point of birthdays. But fear not, sweet Bessie, your fairy gaymother is here to save the day. Hopefully. So in my very best pidgin German – which is dreadful, worse than if an actual pigeon tried to speak German – I start blagging.

My tone is purposeful and business-like. '*Wir* are *hier für* Sex Club,' I insist.

AC doesn't look convinced, but I plough on.

'*Wir* are . . . kinky.'

He scoffs, gesturing at our decidedly unkinky outfits. Although cutting, he does highlight a salient point. We're looking way more department store than dominatrix. In a desperate attempt to demonstrate our kinky credentials, I tug on our bra straps and point emphatically towards them as if to say, 'Look sir, we wear bras and we're not afraid to show you the straps. We are clearly *wild*.' My own wild, sex club bra is a pink, flowery number from M&S.

Luckily, he takes pity on us, or squints a little until he sees our inner sluts, or just can't be arsed to do whatever the hell this is we're doing any more. He nods us through and we cannot believe our good fortune. We are triumphant. Wahey, we're going to the sex club!

'*Danke, danke!*' we cry out in gratitude. '*Gut* sex party to you, sir.'

High on our victory, we pay our entrance fee and totter through to the cloakroom. It immediately becomes clear that before we will be allowed to venture any further into the erotic underworld, we'll have to get our kit off. We obediently disrobe, stripping down to our undies. All around us other people are undressing too, revealing some genuinely showstopping outfits: harnesses, chains, fetishwear, tutus. The club is a strict no phone zone, so we dutifully hand over our mobiles.

There is a clothes check woman, who has already checked in all her own clothes and is now at work in nothing but a crotchless body stocking. She's much friendlier than the security guard. Sealing my dress in a clear plastic bag, she tells me I'm '*zehr attraktive*', which is a thrill, but also a social minefield. How on earth am I supposed to return the compliment? '*Danke,* and you and your fanny look splendid'? I smile shyly, extremely aware that we've only just met and I'm in my pants and she's not wearing pants and I can see her everything and this is A LOT, but hey, I am in sex club world now. This is no time to be prudish.

We head through the doors, hearts pumping, eyes wide and vaginas clenched like steel traps. Inside it's dark and smoky but with bursts of psychedelic colour, strobe lighting and fluorescent paint on the walls. A glitterball hangs from the ceiling. The floors are suspiciously sticky and the air stinks, predictably, of sex. But the diverse crowd is loving it, spanning all ages, genders, body types, sexualities and pain thresholds.

The techno music is throbbing. Other things are throbbing. Oh, I knew it was coming. Everywhere I look, strangers are screwing each other senseless. They are at it hammer and tongs. Part of me is delighted at this scene of sexual liberation. *This must have been what the Sixties were like! Groovy, baby!*

Another part is still on edge and extremely nervous. Suddenly, in this German sex club, I have never felt more British. I applaud all the rampant self-expression, but I'm very sure I don't want to get directly involved in any of it myself. I'm not here for action tonight. My role is as Bessie's chaperone and an accidental, overly polite sexual anthropologist. Imagine Mary Poppins on safari: 'Oh crikey! What a tremendous amount of rutting! Tally ho, good for you. How supercalifragi – no, no, you mustn't use my umbrella for that!'

We grab a drink and head to the dancefloor. I try and fail to look nonchalant, like hanging out with PVC-clad people doing it doggy-style is my idea of a low-key Tuesday. While it takes me a few minutes to chill out and become accustomed to my bold new environment, Bessie is instantly in her element. There's a body painting station, so she gets her chest decorated in fluorescent colours and now her bosom glows in the dark.

She meets a beautiful stranger and now they're kissing and now they're cavorting on this massive four poster bed with no covers. I'm overjoyed for her. This is so exciting! Whoop, whoop, go Bessie! But I also feel very protective and quite maternal. I want her to get off and have a birthday adventure for the ages, but I also want to make sure she is comfortable and safe at all times. I don't usually supervise my friends when they're getting jiggy, but then we aren't usually in a sex club. So, like an embarrassing mama bear gatecrashing her daughter's date, I keep sticking my head around the corner to check in on her, just to make absolutely sure she's still having a marvellous time.

'Are you ok?' I pantomime.

She nods and tries not to giggle at me, her ridiculous friend, popping in for a quick chinwag mid-foreplay.

'Do you want me to stay?' I mouth. Then for clarification,

lest she thinks I am volunteering to be their third, I add, 'For safety.'

She shakes her head and merrily returns to her new lover. I give what I hope is a reassuring, but also right-on thumbs up. As you can tell, I am by far the coolest person in this sex club. Who am I kidding? I'm wearing M&S surrounded by S&M.

With Bessie suitably occupied, I set off to explore. This place is enormous, a labyrinth of dancefloors and darkrooms. There's even a swimming pool. I discover an array of elaborate apparatus and erotic accoutrements including an old dentist's chair, a large cage and a sex swing. With no phone, I lose all sense of time.

Here are some things I see on my travels: spanking (obvs), strap-ons (naturally), gimp masks (bloody loads of them), men being led around on leashes, bondage, flogging, finger-blasting, furious wanking, muff-diving, blow jobs, butt stuff, group sex, gay sex, lesbian sex and even a dash of straight sex (jeez guys, isn't that a bit vanilla?).

When I spot two tattooed women enjoying a heartwarming mutual masturbation sesh in the middle of the dancefloor, I'm genuinely delighted for them. I have to fight the urge to rush over and give them a high-five. I suspect they would leave me hanging. There are plenty of sapphic couples and the odd throuple and I can't help smiling encouragingly at all of them, but it's more 'you go, girls' than 'can I join in?' None of this really turns me on, but somehow all of it sets me free.

Interestingly, this sex club is considerably more respectful than many of the non-sex-club clubs I've been to. The atmosphere is hedonistic and bacchanalian, but there's an emphasis on consent. I clock some suggestive smiles in my direction and I get propositioned a few times, but everyone takes it really graciously when I tell them, 'Thanks, but no thanks. I'm just here to watch.'

I go up to the mezzanine and look down on the mass of writhing half-naked bodies below, some dancing, some making out, some going at it full throttle. This takes people-watching to a whole new level. I have never seen so many strangers orgasm. I'm fascinated and awed by the spectrum of human erotic expression on display. Surrounded by people of all different identities who are having all kinds of encounters, I have a realization. I understand that sex can be whatever you want it to be. It dawns on me that the parameters most people think about sex in are false, constructed limits. Real people have real sex in all different ways and it all counts.

I also clock that the patriarchy is a massive hypocrite, still PRing the shit out of the myth that straight sex is at the top of some manufactured sex hierarchy. Just look at all this awesome, non-straight sex happening around me. People are having a smashing, sexy time and there's barely a heterosexual couple in sight. I learn more about sex that night than I ever did in sex education at school.

*

It's no secret that when school sex ed is so lacklustre, a lot of young people turn to porn for their information. It's also no secret that much of mainstream porn is deeply problematic, featuring overwhelming heteronormativity, the exploitation of sex workers, fetishization of marginalized identities, little mention of consent or contraception and homogenized genitals everywhere you look. In the world of mainstream porn, hairless, surgically altered muffs and giant, veiny schlongs are as commonplace as threadbare plots and unconvincing dialogue. Thankfully, there are an increasing number of queer ethical porn creators making content you can watch and wank to guilt free.

One of the great paradoxes of the male gaze is that, in mainstream porn, the following two things occur simultaneously:

1. We are told that sex needs to involve penetration by a cis male penis to count, ergo sapphic sex isn't real sex.
2. 'Lesbian' is consistently among the most-searched-for terms on porn sites.

Let me get this (not) straight. According to these men, our sex is up there with the sexiest of sex, but it doesn't actually 'count' unless they're watching? They are simultaneously oversexualizing us and undermining the validity of our sex lives.

As for the people who don't consider queer sex to be real sex, how wrong they are. If only they knew just how much queer sex counts. Queer sex can blow your mind and change your life. Queer sex can be healing. It can be hilarious. It can be so hot you can't believe it is actually happening.

What's even more mind-boggling to me is that some of the naysayers decrying the validity of certain queer sex acts are queer themselves. It baffles me that there are some in our community who judge each other's sexual proclivities. Scissor-shamers, I'm looking at you (more on this at the end of this chapter). As long as everyone is a consenting adult, then each to their own, surely? It's also just really misguided for anyone to assume that everyone else is doing it the same way they are.

There is no right way to have queer sex and there is no definitive queer sex act. By liberating us from the confines of the kind of sex that is 'expected' by society, queer sex plugs us right into what we really want. Queer sex can be whatever we want it to be. We define our own desire. Queer sex can be an act of invention, rebellion, empowerment and, crucially, horniness.

As far as I'm concerned, queer sex is The Best Sex. And that's not just me showing off or tooting our horns (something, obviously, we are excellent at). It's scientifically proven. Statistically speaking, sapphic sex is way above average on the satisfaction scale. A 2017 report by The International Academy of Sex Research shows that 86 per cent of lesbian women usually or always orgasm during sex, compared with just 65 per cent of straight women. Obviously, orgasms aren't the be all and end all, but studies back up our suspicion that we really do have a fantastic time in the sack. Which begs the question, just why is our sex so smoking hot? Is it because women know each other's bodies better? Communicate our needs, boundaries and turn-ons more openly? Prioritize each other's pleasure? I suspect it's a saucy mix of all of the above. Our shagging is outstanding and we should be able to celebrate that and reclaim our desire, whatever that looks like.

Scissoring, some thoughts

So here we are. We've reached the point in the book where it is no longer possible for me to resist the urge to talk about the ancient erotic art of the scissor. Buckle up buttercup, because I have a *lot* to say about scissoring.

A debate as old as time

Since day dot, lesbians have squabbled over whether or not scissoring is a thing. Shortly after the original Big Bang, we were quarrelling about whether scissoring qualified as a big bang. In all likelihood, queer cavewomen were debating the existence of scissoring long before scissors were invented. Back then they probably called it Doing the Betty Rubble.

But what is scissoring?

Excellent question, glad you asked. Picture two pairs of open scissors . . . trying to give each other an orgasm. Sorry, was that too abstract? Let's try again. When I was a youngster one of my favourite pastimes was making my Barbies scissor. I'd yank their legs in opposite directions and smoosh their plastic pelvic mounds together until they completely forgot about Ken. Still not totally sure what I'm on about? Ok, imagine you're about to make the beast with two backs with a flexible dreamboat. There you both are, open-minded and open-legged, ready to play an X-rated version of Twister. The aim of the game is to get your bits to make contact with their bits in a way that feels mutually lovely. Congratulations, you are scissoring.

The brutal truth: scissoring might not work

This sad reality contributes to a huge proportion of scissoring-deniers. Sparks may not ignite. You may never achieve lift off. Who hasn't attempted a bit of this scissoring malarkey, started off with high hopes for horny times, then twenty minutes of imprecise, increasingly frustrating frottage later, ended up tangled in a sweaty heap of limbs and regret?

But scissor-shaming still needs to get in the bin

You'd think that the only people who didn't count queer sex as real sex would be straight, but there are in fact a whole host of scissoring-sceptics among the sapphic community. My hunch is that they tried it once, got whacked in the chin by their lover's rogue foot, decided it just isn't anatomically possible and have held a grudge against the concept of scissoring ever since. While it's true that not all combinations of bodies are compatible scissor-wise, a 2012 study in the *British Medical Journal* reveals that 91 per cent of women who sleep with women have scissored. Wondering why your queer pal still hasn't replied to your latest text? Odds are, she's too busy scissoring.

Here is my all-time favourite fun fact about scissoring

It's not only people who scissor. (Please read the rest of this section in your best David Attenborough voice.) Scissoring happens in the animal kingdom as well, especially among female bonobos. Nicknamed the 'Make Love, Not War apes', bonobos are extremely randy. Their most common sexual act? Girl-on-girl tribadism, AKA the humpolympics, AKA scissor time. Anatomically speaking, female bonobos are particularly suited to scissoring because they have – stay with me – humungous clitorises, so prominent they waggle when they walk. How's that for Big Clit Energy? Lady bonobos, I salute you. Experts reckon bonobos scissor, on average, once every two hours. Reports that they have discovered the secret to happiness remain unconfirmed. (Me again.) Sir David! Wait a minute. I thought I wanted to be a professional writer and live a meaningful, authentic life but maybe I just want to . . . be a bonobo?

Can scissoring save the world?

As if bi-hourly scissoring with mega-clits wasn't thrilling enough, bonobos actually use it as a social bonding strategy to forge close connections among the females. That's right. They bond over their love of the rub and form powerful girl gangs so they can stand up to aggressive males. There you have it. Not only is scissoring a thing, it has the potential to destroy the patriarchy. Some people (and the majority of feminist bonobos) scissor, get over it.

CHAPTER 16

This should not be normal

Not to brag but I have had *a lot* of entry level jobs. Receptionist, admin assistant, office coordinator – these are all vital positions that keep companies ticking and the people who do them deserve respect, a lot more respect than we are often given, but they were never jobs that I personally had any desire to do. They do not make me feel fulfilled and the only thing they stretch is my patience for dickheadery. For me, this line of work was intended to be a short-term measure to pay my bills until I landed a steady writing gig, or at least something creative-adjacent. But the stopgap has somehow become my whole CV. I am now twenty-nine. What should have been a mere few months of my professional life has snowballed and I have accidentally been doing clerical and customer service work for over a decade. This realization depresses me deeply.

This is what I'm thinking about in my rather bleak emotional landscape, as I catch the tube to the week-long health and safety course I have to do for my day job. Picture a disillusioned office manager rapidly approaching thirty and even more rapidly losing her patience with all this shit.

Sitting on the underground, I'm half-heartedly scrolling through job boards on my phone, wondering if it's even worth trying any more. I apply for so many positions and never hear back. I pitch articles to editors who never reply. I have no viable contacts, no actionable leads, no clue what I'm doing really. There are certain milestones in life that are meant to mark your ascension to adulthood and I have achieved precisely none of them. No marriage, no partner, no kids, no property-ownership, no financial solvency and no career that doesn't make me feel crap.

For once I'm not crying in a snivelling heap about all this. I am not sobbing on the Central Line. It's not like those turning-thirty meltdowns you see on TV. I'm not Rachel Green in *Friends* bawling about being 'over the hill' while wearing a crown made of cardboard. That's not the vibe at all. This is a lot less noisy and a lot more resigned. It feels like giving up and giving in and life slipping through my fingers. I am depressed and ashamed and so exhausted. All my get-up and go has got up and gone. I am woman; hear me snore. In the grand scheme of life, thirty really isn't very old at all, but approaching this age is a stark reminder of the unstoppable passing of time and all the things I have failed to achieve.

Today I am wondering if being gay has held me back. If all that time spent figuring stuff out and then all those years staying in a relationship that wasn't right for me because, my god, it felt fantastic to finally be with a woman for real, was actually a squandering of youth. I wonder whether if I had felt more confident in my sense of self earlier on, I would have moved more boldly through the world, felt more capable, been more formidable. I wonder if nobody is interested in my voice as a writer, because who wants to hear what some unknown lesbian has to say? Then I wonder if that is all just a bunch of excuses when the real reason for my lack of accomplishment is that I'm simply not cut out for it.

But let's get back to the course, because obsessing over my personal shortcomings isn't going to pay the rent. I arrive at the venue, ready to exchange the mundanity of the office for the mundanity of a workplace training programme. I'm almost looking forward to marathoning cheesy eighties videos featuring amusingly wooden actors with handlebar moustaches, demonstrating how it's a really good idea to not stick your fingers into an open plug socket or carry heavy loads with your arms outstretched like a zombie. I am fully on board the 'bend with your knees' bus.

We complete a module on a topic so scintillating I instantly forget what it was, but I have taken copious notes in my spiral pad so I'm sure it will be fine. Now we're having a five-minute coffee break and I'm sat here sipping knock-off Nescafé from a paper cup, minding my own business, privately staring into the existential abyss. I am currently doing a spot of mental-health-arithmetic. If X is in a job X hates for Y years, how many years will it be before X spontaneously combusts with despair?

I don't know anyone else here. We are a higgledy-piggledy mishmash of strangers from different companies in various industries, united only by our common goals of making our workplaces safer and getting out of the office for a few days. Perched around a large grey table, a few of the attendees make stilted conversation. I don't. So far, I have been polite but not particularly talkative or forthcoming with details about myself. I am not in the mood for chit-chat, so I stay quiet, nursing my dismal cup of coffee and my mounting anguish at the futility of, oh, everything.

Then I hear an exchange that snaps me out of my own head and blasts me right into this present moment. The two men opposite me are talking to each other. I can't remember their individual names. They look confusingly similar. Both wear smart, ironed shirts tucked into smart, ironed trousers. They seem alright, inoffensive if nondescript. I have no strong feelings about either of them. Yet. Then I click into their chat. One of them has just mentioned that there is a lesbian at his work. Suddenly I am all ears.

Smart Shirt 1: 'Of course, you have to be ok with everything these days.'
Tucked Trousers 2: 'Yes.'
Smart Shirt 1: 'But are you . . . ?'
A pause. A look passes between them.
Tucked Trousers 2: ' . . . No.'
Smart Shirt 1: 'Me neither.'

They share another conspiratorial glance, seeming pleased to have found a like-minded peer to do some prejudice with. They have established a mutual bond and reinforced the notion that their bigotry is legitimate because after all, this guy agrees with them. They can't both be wrong, can they?

Then Smart Shirt 1 gets to his feet. He addresses the room.

'Right, let's get back to it, shall we? Next on today's agenda: Diversity in The Workplace.'

Yes, Smart Shirt 1 is our esteemed training coach, here to instruct us on wellbeing at work. He is one of the men who is 'not ok with everything', although he is absolutely ok with voicing his discriminatory views in a room where he is literally being paid to train us on how to behave in our jobs.

When I got dressed this morning, I stupidly forgot to put on my This Is What a Lesbian Looks Like T-shirt. I also neglected to pin a rainbow flag badge to my cardi or get 'DYKE' tattooed on my forehead. What a silly sausage I am. The trainer has no idea that I am a lesbian. He probably thinks that lesbians always look a certain way and, as I don't look that way, it hasn't occurred to him that I might be one of those people he so fundamentally objects to. This is why he feels comfortable enough to be openly homophobic in this room where he is a figure of authority and trust.

I would like to say that this is what happens next: I calmly look him right in the eyes and tell him, in front of everyone, my voice slick with composure and gravitas, 'I'm so glad we're covering diversity next. It is very important to me, as an employee and as (duh, duh, duh!) a lesbian.'

I would also be quite content if I could report that, incensed by this injustice I splutter my mouthful of coffee so it sprays through the air and stains his smart shirt, that I demand to speak to his manager and escalate the incident, so that he is made to feel the consequences of his casual disdain for my identity.

But I do neither of those things. Instead, I sit silently as my vision starts to blur. I am aflame with an avalanche of emotions: righteous indignation, rueful irony, that old familiar shame, coupled with anger that I am the one who feels ashamed when it should be him. I wonder what to do, how to respond, whether to respond. I am aware that my emotional temperature has just skyrocketed. I feel extremely upset and caught off-guard. I know that there are many people who think the same as him. Of course I do. I have encountered homophobia many, many times before, but I hate that in this moment, I am trapped in this room with this man who believes my existence is not ok.

I feel fraught, but I keep my torment internal. I stuff it down inside so that I am railing against him only in my mind, not letting any of that raw, unseemly emotion erupt. I know that if I speak now my voice will tremble or, worse, explode. There is something so triggering about the hypocrisy and the containment and the words he has just spouted mere feet away from me and the fact that I hate my job and I hate having to be with people like him, but I have no viable career alternative and I have bills to pay. If I open my mouth I will either shout or weep. Either way, I will come across as an 'overemotional woman', 'so dramatic', an 'angry, humourless lesbian' in this room full of people I have to spend the rest of the week with. So, I continue in my silent turmoil as this bigot in his smart shirt lectures me on how to ensure my colleagues feel safe to be themselves. 'Diversity in the workplace'? What a fucking joke.

❧

They say receptionists know everything that goes on in a company. Actually, maybe that's not really a saying unless you're part of the receptionist community. But as someone who has womanned many a front desk, I can confirm it is true. We receptionists see and hear it all. We are the gateway to the office and the guardian of all its secrets. We know who has booked which meeting room, how everyone takes their coffee, who came in late and hungover this morning, and who slept with who after the office night out. Bored colleagues stop by our desk and offer up juicy nuggets of scandal, just to kill some time. We carry trays laden with cafetières and carefully arranged biscuits into meeting rooms full of 'important' people talking about 'important' things. We hear stuff. Although we are often the lowest in the pecking order and the pay grade, we become hives of intel on office politics, illicit affairs and inappropriate comments, of which there are almost always an abundance. So I have heard all manner of hideous 'banter', myriad microaggressions and a hell of a lot of blatant, undiluted homophobia. Some of it has been directed at me, some has been in reference to others, and some has just been a strange public venting of rage, scorn or derision.

People might wonder why I never reported any of it to senior management. Well, quite a lot of the time the harassment comes directly from senior management, so that does tend to put a spanner in the works. It is my personal experience that most HR departments, although often staffed by well-meaning personnel, are ultimately there to protect the interests of the employer. Also, I have bills to pay. I do not want to ruffle feathers and mark myself as an office outcast. I do not want to have to deal with the inevitable fallout or be branded an angry dyke who can't take a joke. I just want to get on with my job, collect my pay cheque and figure out how to get the hell out of here for good. So I suck it up, say nothing and make mental notes about who the arseholes are.

Here are just a few of the things I have seen and heard at the various organizations I have worked for over the past decade. There was the all-male senior management team at the advertising firm, who discovered I was a lesbian and proceeded to place bets on which female coworker I was most likely to hook up with, as if my identity was their sport. There was the male CEO in finance who felt the need to tell me he didn't understand 'why gays wanted to be able to get married'. There was the other male chief exec (are we sensing a theme here?) who knew I was gay and still sexually harassed me for months on end, with wandering hands at company functions and wildly inappropriate emails laden with disconcerting innuendos and even more disconcerting winky faces. In one particularly memorable missive he called me his 'concubine, geisha and confidante ;)'.

Much of the homophobia that's been directed my way has been infused into old-fashioned sexual harassment. Particularly heinous was my job on the phones at the catcall centre, where 'the lads from sales' did a lot of 'banter'. Translation? They made obscene comments about female colleagues' bodies and sexualities while sniggering and egging each other on. And of course, there was the usual 'what a waste' nonsense, the sinister gags about 'turning' you, all confidently proclaimed in an open-plan office for everyone to hear. The prejudice so shamelessly on display is grotesque, but it also seems somehow accepted. Verbal sexual harassment is so commonplace in so many of the organizations I work for, it feels like too pervasive and insidious a thing to conquer.

The reality is that men have been saying gross stuff to women at work for centuries. Since I was a teenager, I have experienced sexual harassment in the workplace and it has been completely normalized. It has not been taken seriously. It has seemed that, as a girl and then a woman in junior roles, it was just something I had to put up with. And not only that, I had to be nice to the men who subjected me to this.

So yes, I am sceptical about the much-bandied-about phrase 'corporate inclusion'. Of course, it is vital that companies have policies and procedures in place to protect the physical and mental health and safety of their employees. Of course, organizations must implement and enforce these systems and strive to facilitate a safe environment for their staff. But the existence of documentation and the use of corporate jargon does not ensure the creation of a positive, welcoming workplace. Because workplaces are filled with people and people sometimes behave appallingly. Societal attitudes need to shift, really shift, before there is any hope of stamping out homophobia and misogyny at work.

According to a 2023 study by LGBTQIA business community myGwork, three out of four queer women and non-binary people still fear being totally out at their job. This statistic does not shock me in the slightest. Having a job is hard enough already. Coming out still has the potential to make it a whole lot harder, from navigating prejudice to worrying about career progression.

As I move from dead-end job to dead-end job throughout my twenties, I don't always come out at work, because I fear that it may add another dimension to any unpleasantness. Instead, I do the ninja-like dance of evasion, batting away questions about my love life like tennis balls that could thwack me in the face, avoiding giving specific answers to seemingly innocuous enquiries about what I did at the weekend or whether I have a boyfriend, strictly monitoring what pronouns I use when talking about partners. I don't only employ this strategy at work. I do the same with interactions in my daily life too, sometimes because I can't be bothered with any hassle, sometimes because I'm not in the mood to explain myself, and sometimes because I am scared of what might happen otherwise.

❖

Months after the health and safety course from hell, I am on a night bus returning home to my flat after an evening out with friends. I am alone and have deliberately chosen not to sit on the upper level, a precaution I always take when travelling solo. It is around 2 a.m. and, apart from the driver, I am the only person on the bus. Then a man gets on. I cannot say what he looks like, because I deliberately do not look at him. But I am aware that there is now a man in this space and so I pull my jacket around me tighter, I cross my arms in front of my chest to minimize it, I do not look in his direction. I try and make myself as inconspicuous and unapproachable as possible. These are all small self-adjustments I have made countless times before when in the presence of unfamiliar men, especially at night, especially when I'm alone.

Although there is a bus full of empty seats, the man takes the seat next to me. I continue to stare out of the window. I do not want to make eye contact or any kind of contact with him. But he has other plans.

'Did you have a good night?'

I don't want to encourage a conversation, but I can't ignore him outright when he's this close to me as that might piss him off. I reply in monosyllables.

'Yes.'

I give a tight, quick, false smile. Still, I do not look at him.

'Where you going now?'

'Home.'

'Can I come?' A leering laugh.

I do the tight, quick, false smile thing again, acknowledging that he has made a joke. I keep my head facing away from him, my eyes fixed on the street outside.

'You got a boyfriend?'

At this point I could tell him I'm a lesbian, hoping he'd take the hint and back off, but I suspect he is the type who would only be spurred on by this revelation. From past experience, I know it would almost certainly add another creepy, all-riled-up-got-something-to-prove layer to his advances. So I do not come out to this man. He isn't targeting me because I'm gay. He is targeting me because I am a woman and I am alone and I am vulnerable. But to not come out to this man in this moment is a deliberate choice I make to try and minimize the potential danger of this encounter. I tell him I have a boyfriend, hoping this will be enough to deter him.

No such luck. He doesn't care. Yet still, he persists.

He reaches out and touches my arm. I flinch, shift uncomfortably in my seat. His hand moves to my thigh. I am on high alert now. I don't feel equipped to de-escalate this situation, and it does feel like A Situation, so I have to try and escape instead. I am on the window seat so I must squeeze past him to get out, which feels gross but necessary. Wordlessly, I move to sit at the very front of the bus.

He follows. Of course he does. He starts to speak to me again. His hand is pressing into my thigh. I say nothing. I get up once more and this time I go and stand right next to the driver, so I am in his eyeline. I don't complain about this man to the driver. Maybe this is a mistake, but I am worried that if I do the public accusation might anger the man further. My instinct, as it always has been when I am around a man who makes me uneasy, is defuse, defuse, defuse. Do not engage, do not do anything that might escalate the situation, and for god's sake do not make him cross.

I have been grabbed and groped and had strange men I did not know press their erections against me in a crowd without so much as a hello so many times I have lost count. I do not remember the men's faces, only the way they made me feel. Full of fear and shame and wrongness in my own body. This is far from the first time I have had an encounter with a man that felt unsafe. But there is something here that does feel different, more dangerous, more precarious somehow. Perhaps it is his persistence. The smell of alcohol emanating from him. The unmissable note of aggression in his advances. The fact that it is late at night and the streets are dark and I am all alone. The knowledge that I have nowhere to escape to except the flat where I live on my own.

I really do not want this man to know where I live. I do not want him to know which bus stop is mine. I do not want to ever see him again. I make a split-second decision to get off the bus now before it reaches my usual stop. In one quick movement I slip my shoes off and grab them both in my left hand, my arm pulled protectively across my chest. My keys are in my right hand, pointy end sticking out.

Then I realize that he is getting off the bus too. I am not sporty, have never been sporty, but adrenaline floods my body and now I am running faster than I have ever run in my life. He is following. Now he is saying something, he is shouting something, but I can't hear what because there is blood rushing in my ears. I am being pursued. I am being hunted and I have one driving, primal thought.

RUN. RUN, RUN, RUN, RUN.

This is fight or flight and I am flying as if my life depends on it because maybe it does. Hurtling through deserted streets, I do not know where I am. I only know that I must keep moving. And so I propel myself forwards, forwards, forwards, wherever that may take me.

Eventually I look over my shoulder and he is not there. I keep running for a while longer to be certain. When I am finally sure I have shaken him off, I pause for a second to pull out my phone and find my location on the maps app. I am nearly an hour from home, so I start speed-walking, interspersed with bursts of running when I can manage it. I need to get back to my flat.

And I do. I escape. I make it home. I am one of the lucky ones, but I can feel in my marrow how close a call that was.

When I talk to my friends about it later, still in shock, still shaken up, I find that this experience is familiar to many of them. Like the workplace 'banter' and the creepy bosses and the everyday discrimination and the profound, aching disillusionment in our twenties, it is just what happens to us.

This should not be such a relatable story. None of this should be normal.

Memo

FAO Work colleagues who are struck with a case of lesbian fascination and proceed to ask me invasive questions

Please stop! I get it. You're thinking, 'Ooh, a lesbian. How exotic.' Or perhaps, 'Oh, a lesbian. How odd.' Either way, you're intrigued. You want to know more about us. You want to know *everything* about us, including things that are really none of your business and/or extraordinarily offensive to mention. All decorum flies right out of the window as you become unable to suppress your urge to fire out questions: 'Which one is the man?' 'Have you ever had sex with a man?' 'I know you're a lesbian and everything, but have you thought of this: . . . men?' The thing is, fabulous and interesting we may be, but we still deserve basic manners. We are people, not animals in a zoo to be gawked at or rats in a lab to be (conversationally) probed. So, think before you ask and if there's even the slightest inkling that maybe this isn't the most appropriate thing to say to your LGBTQIA co-worker, here's a thought: don't.

Memo

FAO Work colleagues who are drunk at the office do and desperately want to tell me all their secret sapphic thoughts

Please keep doing this! This might be a controversial opinion and I can't speak on behalf of all queer people, but this is the one reaction to being out at work that I personally quite enjoy. Let's face it, office parties can be a snoozefest. Nothing livens one up quicker than Barbara from accounts accosting me, over-enthusiastic and wild-eyed, dragging me into a corner and confessing that she once had a cheeky snog with her mate Beverly and she still sometimes thinks about it when she's in bed with her husband Barry. Barbara, sweetie, tell me more! Hearing other people's juicy secrets is fun. It's especially fun when a usually buttoned-up co-worker is suddenly spilling out all the details of their sauciest escapades. As long as the person is not offensive, I am very happy to take on the role of a budget lesbian agony aunt, dispensing pearls of sapphic wisdom: 'Only you can know what your dreams about Rihanna really mean, Janet,' etc.

CHAPTER 17

Goodbyes and hellos

The next time I fall in love it happens quite by accident. Oh God, what an *incredibly* annoying thing for me to say. I am rolling my eyes at myself right now. 'When you stop looking, you'll find someone' has to be up there in the hall of fame of hideous things smug partnered-up people tell single people, making said singles justifiably enraged. But, in my case, I'm afraid it's the truth.

I am not searching for another grand romance. I am dating here and there and having the odd brief encounter and that feels about right on that front for now. Besides, I am focusing on more important stuff, like writing and friendships and helping to care for my beloved granny.

She is ailing. Most of the time she is still entirely herself but there are increasing moments of confusion, especially during the night. While rationally I understand that losing your grandparents is a natural part of life, emotionally I cannot bear to think about how much it will devastate me. Because me and my granny? Well, we just adore each other. We listen to each other. We light each other up. She always says to me, 'You do a girl good.' And I understand what she means because she does the exact same thing for me, whether we're gossiping about clothes, or jiving on the living room carpet during *Strictly*, or putting the world to rights over the washing up, her washing, me drying, both of us lingering far longer than necessary over the dishes because we're having such a marvellous time. When we are together, we glow brighter. Our love feels gilded in sunshine.

It is also true that out of all my family, she is the one who received the news about me being gay with the most kindness, the most openness, the most willingness to listen and try to understand. She is the one who greeted my partner with notable warmth and made an effort to make her feel welcome. But most of all, besides all of that, she is my darling girl.

I am in the office one bitter January day when I get the call I have been dreading since I knew what dread was. She is not well. Her condition is deteriorating. I should come now. Thankfully, my work is very good about the whole thing. My boss grants me compassionate leave to go and be with her, for which I am eternally grateful. Even the people at the day job I loathe know how much my granny means to me. I boast about her that often, find excuses to bring up how fabulous she is, regale anyone who will listen with stories of her splendour.

I dash to Kings Cross and catch the next train up north. When I get to her house, she is weak but – thank God – still with us. The following days feel like an alternative reality. I am in a place that is so familiar I know every inch of it. At night when I dream that I am at home, it is Granny's house that I picture. I am surrounded by family I have known all my life, but nothing about any of this feels normal.

She is barely eating, not talking much and frequently in physical agony. I do my best to soothe her suffering, stroking her forehead, reassuring her that the pain will pass. I tell her how much I love her and when she reaches out, childlike, for a hug, I hold her in my arms. Whenever the agony subsides a little, I try to lift her mood. Sometimes it works. I crack jokes and she smiles and it is so beautiful and so bittersweet. I don't know if she will rally. The doctor says not. The doctor says she is on her way out. I google 'signs of dying'. She has most of them, so I have a private weep. Then I pull myself together and return to her side.

One of the signs that haunts me is the hands turning purple as the body starts to shut down and blood circulation dwindles. With Granny, it begins with a bluish hue on the fingertips of her right hand. Over the following hours and days, I obsessively monitor the blue turn to indigo turn to purple and fan out across her delicate skin. Her hands are like icicles and I try so hard to warm them. I take them in mine and rub them under the covers. I stupidly, desperately think that if I can just get her hands warm then maybe I can save her. Maybe then she won't leave me. But of course, it is no use. Her hands will not be warmed. The mottling will not be stopped. It spreads across her palms and down her forearms, like macabre blossom. And then, with quiet, contained horror, I see the creeping colour on her left fingertips.

❋

It is now Friday afternoon and I have just woken up from a snatched nap. My body and brain are utterly exhausted after I stayed up all last night with her. I check in on her now. She seems stable. I am so bone-weary I wonder about staying in my pyjamas, but quickly decide against that. It might seem strange to her if I am in my nightwear. Besides, I always dress up when I'm seeing my granny. So I dress for her as I have done so many times before. I pull on a vintage wrap sweater and a pair of high-waisted cigarette trousers in dark green tartan I know she particularly likes. I tidy my hair and I fix my face and I head back into her room.

Her condition starts to significantly deteriorate. It seems that the end is approaching. Instinctively, without having discussed it beforehand, my mum and I become the perfect double act for this moment. We are either side of our matriarch, my mum holding her right hand and me holding her left. My mum does brilliantly, gently guiding her through relaxation techniques to soothe her agitation.

Then I come in with the words. I know exactly what words to say because I know how to make her feel good. I always have done and I do right now. I tell her how loved she is, how she is the belle of every ball. I do a sort of improvized *This Is Your Life* speech, recapping all the highlights, all the glamour, all the good, lovely, warm things. I should say that this is not my original idea. I cannot take credit for its majesty. My granny did a similar thing when she saw my grandad out of this world. I was at university at the time, but I was the one who stayed with her that awful night after he passed. It was just the two of us. We talked and we wept and she told me how it had been and what she had said to him. So really, she is the one who taught me how to say the very best goodbye. And now, I am saying it to her.

I tell her how much I adore her, how much everyone adores her, how it is impossible not to adore her because she is so undeniably adorable. I show her the photo of her and my grandad on their wartime wedding day, him dashing in his army uniform, her impossibly young and gorgeous in a gown of white lace. I tell her the truth: that in all my life I have never seen anyone look at another person with such unadulterated devotion as the way he looked at her.

As she starts to fade further, I stop calling her Granny. I use her first name instead. This is about her, not me, and even if she doesn't remember who I am or that she has grandchildren or even children, she will know the important thing: that she is safe and she is loved.

I am holding her hand the moment she passes. She dies with a smile on her face. I do not mean that figuratively and I swear I am not exaggerating. That really is how she goes. Even in death, she is spectacular. She takes one final breath. A beam spreads wide across her lips. She is radiant for one last moment on this Earth. Her heart flutters for the final time in her chest.

And then she is gone.

In my frantic googling, I have read that some people think hearing might be the last thing to go, even after the breathing has stopped, so I keep on talking to her, gently, lovingly. If any part of her is still conscious I do not want her to hear anything distressing, like sobbing or frightening words about her being dead. I want her to keep hearing only soothing, comforting words. I want her to keep feeling the strength and softness of my love, so that is what I give her.

I manage to remain quite composed until the undertakers come and carry her body away. I watch it happen. My mum says she needs to watch, that this is part of accepting that she really is gone, and I can't let my mum watch this alone. So we stand together. And then she is gone. And that is when I break. That night my mum and I sleep in the same bed in her childhood bedroom, the room I always slept in when I stayed over, right next to Granny's.

In the coming days and weeks and months and years, I feel self-conscious about the magnitude of my grief for my granny. I have lost family members before and it was awful, but I have never experienced anything quite this enduringly horrendous. For many, losing a grandparent is a sad but manageable, fathomable fact of life. For me, it is like one of the Earth's tectonic plates has dropped out from under me. It is as if part of me, the purest, most hopeful, most joyful part, has been extinguished forever. I feel irrevocably altered by both my love for her and the loss of her.

I know that holding her hand and seeing her off was the hardest but most important thing I've ever done. And actually, it wasn't the hardest. The hardest is what comes afterwards. The hardest is living with the knowledge that I will never see her again. The knowledge that whatever happens in my life, good or bad, I won't be able to tell her about it. The knowledge that I will never again experience the glow of our gilded sunshine love. Every night when I go to sleep, I will myself to dream of her. Some nights I succeed and when I do, I hug her so tight and tell her over and over how much I love her. And then I wake up and remember she isn't here any more.

Back in London, in my flat alone, I pore over photographs as 'Close To You' by The Carpenters plays on repeat. I notice that in nearly every picture of us together we are either beaming or gripped in conversation, riveted by whatever the other is saying. I remind myself that I should be grateful for the time we had. I remind myself that grief is the price we pay for love, and that my grief is only this vast because of the scale of our love. I remind myself that the best way to honour her is to keep her spirit alive, channelling her irresistible charm, humour and sparkle in my own life. She is part of me. She shaped the fabric of who I am. I must hold on to that. And then I think about how, within the space of two short years, I have lost two of the most defining women of my life. One through a break-up, the other through bereavement. But if I thought the pain of the end of my relationship was bad, it is dwarfed in comparison to this heartbreak.

❧

So this is the emotional state I am in. It's the week after she passed away and I'm back at work, trying not to cry all over the guests. I am looking for a distraction, but I discover a woman who becomes more than that. And where do I find her?

Say hello to our old friend, Gaydargirls.com.

Where else would I look for content outrageous enough to distract me from my anguish, other than my GDG inbox? When the site loads, I see that I have a new message. I open it up. Four words.

'I love red lipstick.'

I click on the sender's profile and there's a photograph of a woman with dark hair, dimples and the dreamiest big brown eyes I've ever seen. She's hot. She likes red lipstick. This could be just the distraction I need. I reply and she gets back to me almost immediately. We swap dating stories. She jokes that she's met a few friends, but not yet found anyone who wants to marry her. I take the bait and ask if she's building up to pop the question to me. Her response?

'You only get a marriage proposal if I get your number.'

Once upon a WhatsApp

Roxy: Hi hello. It's me! It's not flirt divert!

Naomi: Haha, phew 💍 There you go 😊

Roxy: It's beautiful. I love it

Naomi: Blimey, this was easy

Roxy: Think I should wait until I've met you in person to give you my answer though

Naomi: Not so easy

Roxy: So close

Naomi: Damn it

Roxy: I can't say yes if I've never met you. Also. You are suspiciously eager to find a wife. Is this for visa reasons? Or just because there are so few gay women in your village, you need to import some?

Naomi: A little from column A, a little from column B. I just thank my lucky stars I'm not coming off as desperate. I could really screw this up

Roxy: Do you normally propose this early on in a conversation? It's like you're flyering but for marriage

Naomi: I'm not sure there is a correct answer for this. This is all going wrong 🙈 Not so smooth after all. Who knew?!

Roxy: You're doing fine. So would you consider yourself a ladies' lady?

Naomi: How do you mean? A slapper?

Roxy: I meant because you've referred to yourself as smooth

Naomi: I've been single for two years, can't be that smooth

Roxy: You might just like being single

Naomi: I hate being single

Naomi: I mean yes, that's it 😄

Roxy: What's your type?

Naomi: Femme, confident and curvy. What's yours?

Roxy: I get really turned on by women who come on too strong and propose to me before we've even met

Naomi: Excellent, me and you are going to get on

Roxy: Haha. My type . . . It sounds silly but I think just beautiful, strong women. Doesn't have to be physical strength. Inner strength does it for me too

Naomi: I'm strong like bull 💪

Naomi: You want me to add you on FB? I warn you, you'll want to block me from your feed quite quickly

Roxy: Go for it

Naomi: Yep, you are HOT. Confirmed

Roxy: Is that why you wanted to be my Facebook friend? To verify hotness?

Naomi: Haha, yes, I mean no, I mean yes

Naomi: You passed, let's just be happy 😊

Roxy: Are you superficial, Naomi?

Roxy: Also, woohoo – I passed!

Naomi: Very

Naomi: Kidding, kidding

Roxy: Hahaha

Naomi: It's just a bonus that you are hot. I'd still chat to you if you weren't such a looker. I wouldn't ask you out on a date though. Would you like to go out on a date?

Naomi: THAT 👆 has got to be THE most romantic thing I have EVER said

CHAPTER 18

How to fall in love when your heart is broken

Naomi pulls up in her car outside my flat on a cold, sunny Friday in February. She is wearing a leather jacket, aviators and a shy smile. She has driven all the way from the Midlands to London specifically for this date. When she google-mapped my address and noticed that it was around the corner from Nutter Lane, she was understandably concerned. But then again, there is only one other lesbian in her village and she's already been out with her.

Before we meet in person, she insists on a phone call. She suspects I might be a catfish, which I take as a compliment. I am excessively anxious about this call. Phone calls in general give me anxiety. But I do want to go on a date with her and I do live near Nutter Lane, so it's fair enough that she wants to safeguard. When we speak, we get on immediately. She is warm and witty and sweet, and I am sufficiently non-nutter-like to secure that crucial first date. We agree that she will drive to mine and we'll go for drinks and dinner. She offers to book a hotel room, but I tell her not to worry. She can stay at my place. Warning: this is not a safety-first approach to dating. I should definitely know better and so should she. But I feel bad she's spending all that money on petrol and, to be frank, I want to get laid. I want to stop living in my aching, mangled heart, and exist for one night only in my body.

Back to the date. As she is closing the car door with one hand, I see that in her other hand she holds flowers. A lush, full bunch of hot pink roses, the exact same shade as the ones at my granny's funeral. I do not put much stock in signs from the universe, but the roses feel symbolic.

As I show Naomi inside, I thank her for the beautiful flowers without telling her why they are so poignantly beautiful to me. I have already made a pact with myself that I will not talk about Granny's death on this date. I do not want to dwell in my emotions today. On the contrary, I am searching for a distraction from the chasm of my grief. The vibe I'm striving for is fun and flirty. If I open that particular door I can't guarantee I'll hold myself together, let alone remain fun and flirty. Sobbing woman does not exactly say seductive minx.

Inside my tiny flat, I pour us some pink wine and locate a tall glass to use as a makeshift vase. I need to trim the bouquet, so I clamber on my bed and stand on tiptoes to retrieve a pair of scissors from the shelf. I am unaware that this act of reaching hoicks the hem of my dress skywards, revealing the top of my stockings and the bottom of my bottom. I know, I know. I'm a walking *Carry On* film. I will not find out that I have flashed her within five minutes of meeting her until the next day. Unused to this level of risqué behaviour, Naomi suddenly becomes extremely nervous and starts knocking back booze with haste. That poor, terrified, country lesbian.

Perching on the chaise longue, we talk and drink and flirt. Our chemistry is palpable from the start. She is very funny and I really fancy her. She's even better looking than her pictures on Gaydargirls. Not to toot my own trumpet, but I can tell she fancies me too. It is written all over her lovely, increasingly squiffy, face. As I gaze into her big brown eyes with their dreamy long lashes, I have one thought.

She's wankered! If she carries on like this, there's no way I'm getting any tonight!

I tactically suggest we head out for some sobering night air and get something to eat. We walk the fifteen minutes to the local high street and find a hipster-ish pizzeria. She is smashed, but also smashing. Literally. Trying to be all debonair, she reaches across the table and accidentally knocks the glass candle holder, which smashes to pieces on the floor.

'Food!' I say brightly. 'Let's get you some food.'

Post-pizza, back at mine and sobered up, we sit on my bed. Finally, we kiss and it's electric. Kissing leads to more than kissing. She stays the night, but neither of us gets much sleep.

Usually when getting naked with someone new, I'd be fretting about whether she'll fancy me in the buff. In this instance I am unusually confident that she will like what she sees. This is not due to me suddenly becoming a massive-headed egomaniac. It is because I have evidence.

Prior to our date, I'm looking through Naomi's Facebook photos when I stumble across an image from two years ago that stops me in my scrolling tracks.

A snowman. A snowwoman to be precise, painstakingly sculpted by Naomi's fair hands. She has the dimensions of a plus size Jessica Rabbit, an hourglass rendered entirely in frost.

Bloody hell. She's made me out of snow.

It is preposterous how much this ice queen is my doppelganger. She really is my cold-blooded twin, from her long hair with the sweeping side fringe to those humungous slush puppies. The only difference I can spot is that her arms are made out of twigs. If anything, this blizzard bombshell is bigger than me. Wahey! I've got several dress sizes to play with and I'll still, presumably, be Naomi's dream girl. Suddenly, I feel like I'm starring in a low-budget lesbian Christmas romcom. A bizarre sapphic remake of *The Snowman*, where a lonely, country lesbian is so desperate to find love in winter, she builds her fantasy woman out of snow. The snow queen melts. She is crestfallen . . . until she miraculously comes to life again on Gaydargirls!

When I show my friends the photo, they piss themselves laughing. The resemblance really is uncanny. I cannot over-state how much discovering the sexy snowwoman delights me. It's demonstrating Naomi's creativity, her sense of humour and, most reassuringly of all, that I embody her phys-ical ideal. Like the snowwoman herself, my body image angst just melts away. I am confident that I am very much her type, so much so she'd spend hours sculpting me out of snow, presumably risking quite serious frostbite.

Our courtship moves fast. In a classic lesbian power move, Naomi insists we go exclusive after the first date. I'm not especially looking for anything serious. My primary objective is to distract myself from my pain, to feel something, anything else. But I say sure. After all, she is great in bed and, I reason, if I only sleep with one woman at a time it will significantly reduce my dating admin.

After our spicy first encounter, she is concerned that I am just after sex. She is not entirely wrong. She tells me, in no uncertain terms, that on our second date there can be abso-lutely no hanky panky. I agree to this, reassuring her that of course I'm happy to just spend time getting to know each other, while quietly thinking, 'Bet we have sex.' Lo and behold, I am proved right.

On our second date I also tell Naomi about my granny. I show her my favourite photos and try to put into words how marvellous she was. She listens attentively and tells me about the ones she's loved and lost. As we get to know each other, I learn her story too, what matters to her, what makes her tick. Outwardly, we're very different. She is tall. I am short. She is a self-proclaimed butch. I am full-throttle femme. She has always lived in a village. I'm a lifelong city-dweller. She does half marathons. I actively avoid being active. She loves to cook. I can barely boil an egg. Yet somehow our temperaments match. We make each other laugh, delighting in our shared sense of silliness. We get each other.

A long-distance love story, we see each other most week-ends. Either she races down the M1 to mine or I catch the train or the coach up to hers. Our song is Cyndi Lauper's 'I Drove All Night'. The early Monday mornings so we can get back to our respective jobs are brutal, so we routinely trudge into work like a pair of sleep-deprived zombies. Then during the week, I am fizzing with anticipation, desperate to see her, frustrated she lives so far away. I find myself wishing weekdays away, not only because my unhappiness at work is increasingly grinding me down, but also because I just want to get to the part where I am back in her arms and in her bed.

✿

We've been together for a few months now and I want to give lovely Naomi a lovely surprise. So far, so good. But then we get to the particular surprise I have in mind. For some reason, I have got it into my head that it would be a brilliant idea to turn up at her house wearing nothing but a basque, stockings and a flasher mac. I have not factored in that this sort of caper only really works in low-budget pornos and bonkbusters by Jackie Collins. Neither have I properly understood the implications of dressing like a 1980s femme fatale on the Megabus. But what do I care of cramped conditions and potential public humiliation via accidental flashing? I am a slightly deranged woman on a slightly deranged mission. Let's do this. Commencing Operation Supervixen.

Getting ready at home, I wiggle into my raunchy undercrackers, button up my trench coat to avoid giving the driver a heart attack and check out my reflection in the mirror. Not too shabby. But give me a couple of hours on a low-cost coach and let's see how shabby I am. It is an extremely tense tube ride to the coach station. I stupidly forgot that it's always summer on the Central Line. The lack of air conditioning is making me all hot and bothered, and not in the way I'm hoping to make Naomi hot and bothered, the poor, oblivious girl. Right now, I am one sweaty Betty. But I can't exactly whip off my coat in front of all these people who, notably, are not my gorgeous new squeeze. Oh dear. My saucy master plan is already going awry.

Finally, I make it to Victoria station. My make-up is slightly smudged, but nevertheless I'm ready to board the love bus. I mean the Megabus. I silently pray for a whole two-seater to myself. My prayers are not answered. So now I'm next to Josephine Blogs, who keeps giving me peculiar side-eye glances. Can she tell what I'm wearing under my mac? Does she have X-ray vision? Oh, mind your beeswax, Josephine. We've all got to get our kicks somehow. It's not exactly the comfiest of coach attire, but at least barely being able to breathe means my nostrils are less stung by the Megabus's famed Eau D'Armpit.

SCREEEEECH!!

A sudden emergency stop. We have a high-risk situation on our hands. Boob-alert! Repeat: we have a Code Red boob-alert!

Phew, that was close. My Megabust very nearly Megaburst right out of my Megabasque. I'm less Sophia Loren, more *Carry On Up The Coach*.

At long last, I arrive at Naomi's front door. It's been an odyssey, but here I am. Let's do a quick check before I go in. Flasher mac? Check. Basque still in place? Just about. Hair and make-up looking fabulous? Not really, but at this point, who cares? Ooh, she's opening the door. I just know she is going to be bowled over. All the stress and discomfort will have been worth it. I am a powerful seductress. Operation Supervixen: mission complete!

She opens the door. She takes in my ensemble. I look at her face, expecting it to be overcome with desire. Instead, she looks concerned. 'You went on the coach dressed like that?!'

✻

Another Friday night I turn up at hers, dressed in my normal clothes. Submerged in my own sadness, I feel like a shell of a person. I am terrible company. Monosyllabic at first. Then one glass of wine in, weeping uncontrollably on her sofa.

Faced with a snivelling human husk where her saucy new minx should be, Naomi takes the most delicate care of me. She holds me as I heave with sobs. She doesn't pressure me to talk or get annoyed that I'm spoiling our time together. She understands and she does not judge.

She runs me a bath, lights aromatherapy candles, plays Eva Cassidy on Spotify and sits with me as I soak my tears away. She listens while I spill out all my jumbled, dark, painful thoughts. When I am emotionally spent, she wraps me up in her bed and brings me a homecooked meal. It is all so gentle and caring and comforting. I have never experienced such tenderness.

I've always felt self-conscious about the size of my emotions. Forever worried about being too much. But now my pain is too raw to play down. My wounded animal self is exposed. What is interesting, what is new, is that she is not put off by my unbridled emotional outpourings. She stays with me. She makes me feel safe to express all the pain I feel. And so, she sees not just my seductive, witty, palatable side, but also the behind-closed-doors of my primal, messy grief. I ask if it scares her. She says no. She says it shows her that I am a person who loves deeply, and that she is the same way.

It is a strange thing to be simultaneously mourning a profound loss and embarking on a new romance. Falling for someone while falling apart. I suppose it is proof that life really does go on, even if it feels that bit heavier and bleaker than before. This moment in time when I meet her, I am at my lowest point. And yet here, in the depths of my despair, I find the start of something beautiful.

It is love at first sight . . . for Naomi. For me, that part takes a little longer. I'm so consumed by grief and burned by my last relationship, I'm hesitant to give my heart away again easily. I have privately resigned myself to the idea of ending up an old maid, hopefully with an apartment in Paris, a collection of glamorous loungewear and a string of dynamic lovers. But in time, I do fall in love with Naomi. I find that, despite what I had believed, miraculously, there is more love in this world for me.

It is a different love to my first love. I know myself better now, understand my needs and my sensitivities, and communicate both. I would say it's a more grown-up love, but as we are the daftest of goofballs together on a daily basis, I don't know if I could keep a straight face on that one. And when I do finally fall for her, it is exquisite and it is terrifying. Because what if I lose this love too? What if everything gets messed up all over again?

❀

Even though I have interacted with human beings before and it's gone fine, I am incredibly nervous about meeting Naomi's family for the first time. We've been together for ten months and while the rest of my life is a disaster, the relationship is going brilliantly. Too brilliantly. So brilliantly I am convinced I'm going to do something to screw it up. I'm desperate to make a good impression at this meal, especially with her parents, Angela and Mark. I tell Naomi I'm worried, but she reassures me that they will love me, because she does.

Mark is a culinary connoisseur. I am not, but I don't want him to find that out. So here I am in this restaurant, drinking wine I can't stand that will probably give me a headache and saying things like, 'Oh Mark, this is really something.'

Now I find myself eating an oyster, trying to impress him with how refined my palate is, despite the fact that seafood makes me queasy. 'Mmm, great oysters here, Mark!' I enthuse, while praying I don't gag on the slime that's just slipped down my throat.

I am so nervous, it's making me act a bit weird. Not with them, thank god. With them, I am charm personified. I'm afraid to say it's poor Naomi who bears the brunt of my crackerjack side.

When we're alone together in the ladies, she grins at me. 'See! It's going great. Are you feeling more relaxed now?'

'Don't be ridiculous!' I snap, in a highly strung whisper. 'I am incredibly tense!' In case there is any doubt I add sharply, 'I will not relax all night!'

Then back to the table I go, to continue my performance in the role of 'normal person'.

At the hotel that evening, it's just the two of us again. I can't deny the meal went well. There is no sane reason for me to have a meltdown. But I have one anyway.

I know I'm overreacting and making a giant fuss over

nothing, but I can't stop myself spiralling. I've just had a crashing realization that I really, really want Naomi's parents to like me, because I really, *really* love their daughter. Just how much I love her, and how important her parental approval feels, is scaring the bejesus out of me. I haven't felt this strongly about anyone since my last relationship and that ended so, so badly.

In a tizz, I think to myself, 'This was only supposed to be an internet date and a one-night stand. How has this got so out of hand?!'

But here we are. I am crazy about this woman, and it's making me act crazy in front of her. I need to buck my ideas up and pull myself together. I would hate to jeopardize what we have. Which is ironic, because my behaviour right now can't exactly be appealing.

But the thing I've only just fully understood is how startlingly into her I am. She's the ultimate trinity: kind, funny, beautiful. I feel like I've hit the jackpot, and that makes me panic that it's bound to implode. I'm not meant to get a happy ever after. I've always presumed I'd end up a slightly tragic, fabulously dressed spinster. I've been with Naomi for almost a year and I'm still in shock that the relationship is going so well. Surely, I'll do something to mess it all up soon. Some self-destructive impulse will rear its head and the whole thing will be ruined. Maybe my bizarre meltdown will be what destroys us.

She looks at me like I'm acting nuts, which, to be fair, I am.

'Yes, I can see why you're so upset,' she jokes. 'Having a lovely meal with nice, friendly people. I'd be upset too.'

Naomi's phone pings. It's a text from her mum. Oh god. Angela is the one I want to like me the most. Naomi's very close to her and I genuinely really liked her too. She was so sweet and touchingly emotional about her family. I brace myself as Naomi starts to read the message aloud.

'Roxy was fantastic company. Fitted in perfectly. Felt like I'd known her for years.'

Say what now? Did I just get a rave review from the MVP?!

After that, I'm completely normal again.

I'm just a girl, standing in front of a girl, asking her to forgive my irrational breakdown.

I soon become close to Naomi's parents. I stop acting so weird. And they embrace me warmly as one of the family.

As for my parents, Naomi doesn't meet my dad, but she does meet my mum. How does that go? Not brilliantly. My mum deliberately and repeatedly calls Naomi by the wrong name. She mixes it up a bit in terms of exactly which wrong name she uses. Sometimes she addresses her as Natalie, at other times Nadine. Frankly, I'm surprised she doesn't just call her Rupert. Natalie/Nadine/Rupert handles the whole thing like a champ, responding dutifully to whatever name my mum decides to use at any given time. This stubborn refusal by my mum to call Naomi by her actual name continues for the first three years of our relationship.

Postcards from a second-chance romance

March: *Beaches*

You are shocked that I have never seen *Beaches*. 'How can this be?' you wonder aloud as you locate the DVD and press play. As you have seen *Beaches* before, years ago, almost immediately you fall asleep. In doing so you leave me, a *Beaches* virgin in the throes of grief, flying solo at the mercy of *Beaches*. The laughter. The heartbreak. The bit where Bette Midler dresses up as a giant bunny. As the closing credits roll, you stir from your slumber to find me bawling my eyes out. 'Oh shit,' you say. 'I really didn't think this through.' You apologize profusely.

April: *Wicked*

I want to treat you to a night out in London's glittering West End, so I splurge on two tickets to see *Wicked the Musical*. We turn up at the Apollo Theatre, glowing with the romance of our big date night. Only then do I realize there are in fact two Apollo Theatres in town and I have taken us to the wrong bloody one. It's curtain-up in fifteen minutes and curtain-down on any delusions I had that I could pull off a great date. I am an idiot. You sweep in and save the day, flagging down a taxi. We arrive in the nick of time. You are a lesbian knight in shining denim.

May: Girlfriend

I am drunk and you are trying to convince me to be your girlfriend. We've been exclusive since our first date. I don't want to be with anyone but you, but I am still resistant to the 'girlfriend' label. It makes me nervous. Using it didn't work out well for me last time. 'Oh, go on,' you say. 'We're basically girlfriends already.' You have a point and you are so pretty. I say yes. I still feel the same when I'm sober.

June: Friends
You meet the girls at an art deco bar in Camden. You are warm and witty and they like you straight away. It possibly helps that you buy them drinks all night. Well played.

July: Paddling pool
One hot summer's day in an attempt to lift my spirits and bring the Costa Del Sol to Ashby-de-la-Zouch, you set up an inflatable paddling pool in your back garden. I don a 1950s bikini. You produce a jug of Pimm's and I cheer. It is ridiculous and you are so lovely.

August: Weeping
Sad day today. Granny's birthday. You hold me in your arms as I fall to pieces.

September: Paris
You whisk me away to the city of light for my thirtieth birthday. You've booked us three nights in the Marilyn Monroe hotel. Our room is all black-and-gold old-school glamour, inspired by a bottle of Chanel No. 5. We watch world-famous cabaret at the Crazy Horse. A row of immaculate, scantily clad dancers with matching bobs high-kick in unison. I wear a red dress and the jewellery Granny left me. Of course, this is all too perfect for words, so fate intervenes and gives me a cold. I am sniffly, but happy. You bring me macarons from McDonald's.

October: Future

I hop on a train mid-week to see you, because I miss you so much. We decide to move in together and you start searching for a job in London. Yes, it will be cramped in this teeny tiny bedsit, but I cannot wait to live with the woman I love.

CHAPTER 19

Something must change

While my love life is going wonderfully, my work life has never felt more hopeless. Hot, faint and headachy, I'm on the tube on my way to the office and dreading the day ahead as usual. I've had to drag myself to get this far. There are no available seats, so I'm stood uncomfortably, jammed in with my fellow commuters. I've popped two painkillers, but they're not even touching the sides. My temples are throbbing violently. The pain rips through my skull. My eyesight starts to blur around the edges Wavy little lines of light appear, flicker and warp. My vision seems to fizzle. I'm going to be sick. I try to breathe deeply, try to regain self-control, but this is frightening. Panicking, I get off the train at the next station, stumble over to the wall and feel my way down it until I'm slumped on the floor. By now my whole vision is pixelated. It's like I'm looking through a kaleidoscope. I do not make it to the office today.

In the six months since I turned thirty, strange health-related things like this have been happening with increasing regularity. Angry red rashes flaring up on my skin. Pains, so many pains, gripping my back and neck and gut. Bouts of vertigo so bad I literally can't walk in a straight line without toppling over. And the skull-crushing migraines that crop up without warning, sending me temporarily blind. It is all very odd, unusual, unsettling.

There is a stark contrast between how I feel at home with Naomi (grieving and struggling, but comforted and held) and how I feel at work (frustrated, desperate, unable to withstand a moment more). Losing my granny also reminds me of the brevity of our time on Earth. It makes me take stock of where I am and highlights how far that is from where I want to be. I've always told myself I'm staying in these dead-end jobs because I have to pay my rent. But is it really that I'm scared I don't have what it takes to succeed in a creative career? Now Naomi's moved in, my rent has never been lower. She urges me to quit and find a job that makes me happy. We can cover the rent between her wage and my bits of freelance work in the meantime. So what is it that's stopping me? Could it be the fear of failure?

Wrestling with all this, on top of the grief, is taking its toll on my physical and mental health. Overwhelmed by negative thoughts, I'm having dark days and even darker nights. I regularly wake up at 2 a.m., breathless, sweaty and terrified from one of my chronic, harrowing nightmares. Too rattled to close my eyes, I lie there till dawn and worry. I start to fear bedtime. Of course, the lack of sleep makes everything so much worse.

Throughout my life I have wrestled with anxiety, low mood and even lower self-esteem. That stuff has always been there, a backdrop to my existence. I never quite know whether it's just part and parcel of being a person, or something more serious. So far, these problems have mostly remained at an unpleasant yet manageable level. By that I mean that although I have regularly felt like I hated the world and detested myself most of all, I have still mostly been able to function in society. When things get tough, I've either slapped a smile on in public, then crumbled to pieces in private afterwards, or withdrawn for a while, cancelled plans and hidden away until the fog has lifted.

But now the weight of my grief has ground me down. I am less resilient and have less hope than I used to. And maybe being with Naomi, someone who will hold me steadily as I fall apart, has allowed me to break so wide open it's all come flooding out.

It feels like thirty years of not-properly-processed pain is finally catching up with me and it's all too much. The grief. The heartbreak. The rejection. The bitter disappointments. The misogyny. The microaggressions. The power-tripping bosses. The catcalls. The dickheads. The homophobes. The hiding. The barely surviving pay cheque to pay cheque. The devastating futility of it all. Thirty years of constantly feeling like I'm failing. That I am not enough. Not successful enough. Not slim enough. Not straight enough. And the shame. Thirty years of self-hating, corrosive, white-hot shame.

Naomi is supportive and caring, but still the landscape of my mind is not a happy place to be. My misery is mounting, morphing into something more sinister and self-destructive. I am fraying, emotionally, physically. I am starting to come apart at the seams.

I go to the doctor, relay my symptoms, take blood tests. The diagnosis? Stress. The prescription? Avoid stress. Something has to change. I am no longer just a bit down; I am heading for a breakdown.

✳

Sometimes it seems like mental health issues are almost expected to happen in queer people. There's a term. 'Minority stress': the particularly high levels of stress faced by those with stigmatized marginal identities. Is it any wonder so many of us have anxiety and depression when we live in a world that consistently others us? The 1987 British Societal Attitudes Survey showed that 75 per cent of the population believed same-sex relations were always or mostly wrong. Only 11 per cent thought they were not wrong at all. I was two at the time. That is the world, the society, I was born into. Section 28 only reinforced the stigma and so-called conversion 'therapy' is still legal in the UK in 2024.

Stonewall's 2018 LGBT In Britain Health Report revealed that more than half of LGBTQIA people surveyed had experienced depression in the past year; 60 per cent of lesbians and 72 per cent of bi women had experienced anxiety. And devastatingly, 31 per cent of lesbian, gay and bi people, and 46 per cent of trans people, had considered taking their own life. But it's not our identities that are making us ill. It's the way the world responds to them.

Yet there's this damaging idea that our sexuality or gender identity is a mental health issue in itself. The World Health Organization only declassified homosexuality as a mental illness in 1993. I was eight. That stuff all seeps in. Media portrayals of 'crazy lesbians' and 'batshit bisexuals' don't help. When I think back to the scant media representation I saw growing up, there was a disproportionate number of murderous bi women and dykes behind bars, reinforcing the stereotype that queer women are inherently obsessive, unhinged and dangerous, when actually, it's society's discrimination against us that amplifies our mental health concerns.

It's an area that urgently needs attention, but despite the stark statistics, it is still not seen as a priority. For the mental health disparity between straight and queer people to change, really change, we need to dismantle the patriarchal systems that oppress us. A daunting task, but an essential one. We need more positive representation to shift societal attitudes, training for healthcare professionals to equip them to treat LGBTQIA patients, and more funding for mental health services for all, including our community.

✣

After one particularly heinous day at work, my own mental health issues come to a head. Telling Naomi about another awful shift somehow swells up into an emotional meltdown. There is, I'm ashamed to say, some very unattractive howling. She has seen me upset before, but this is undignified even for me. She is naturally concerned.

Once again, she urges me to quit. My friends offer the same counsel. Get out. Move on. Make a change. Feeling desperate, I ramp up my job search. Maybe a fresh start will help sort me out. And then I see it, a gift from the gay gods. There's an advert for an entry-level position at my favourite lesbian magazine. A magazine I've read since I was a closeted, teenage lesbian in Leeds. DIVA is looking for an editorial assistant.

The application process is full on. As well as submitting my CV and cover letter, I have to make a social media video, create an image for Instagram, Facebook and Twitter, and write a feature. I rope my friends in to appear in the video. I toil over my application for days, obsess until every detail is as perfect as I can make it. Nervously, I press send on the email with its many attachments, including my hopes and dreams.

A week passes by. I don't hear anything. Then another week. Still nothing. Then suddenly, ping! An email from DIVA's editor inviting me for an interview.

Fireworks! Excitement! Air punching!

This feels like something. A glimmer of hope. A vote of confidence. Evidence that my creative work must be worth something after all.

On impulse, I quit my day job. Not because I am certain

I'll get the *DIVA* gig, but because it's clear my health can't take being here any more. I need to take the leap and leave. Besides, just getting this interview has bolstered my confidence. If I don't get the job, I'll keep applying for writing gigs, ramp up my freelance bits and temp if I need to.

I've been fantasizing about quitting forever. I have quitting anthems with various degrees of rage. Hepburn's 'I Quit', Florence & The Machine's 'Dog Days Are Over', Lily Allen's 'Fuck You'. The reality of quitting is disappointingly anti-climactic. I ask to speak to my line manager in private and tell her I'm handing in my notice. Cold-eyed, she nods. 'I had a feeling. It's bad timing.' The whole meeting lasts about one minute.

But there's no time to dwell in negativity now. I have a life-changing interview to prepare for. I pore over back issues of *DIVA*, brainstorm content ideas and do forensic research into the LGBTQIA community, culture, activism, everything queer I can find. What are *DIVA* readers interested in? What do they care about? What are their pain points? What questions are they asking? What do they need to know?

The interview itself is intense. The magazine's core writing staff of three sits across the table from me like a queer version of *The X Factor*. They take it in turns to fire out questions.

'The *DIVA* website is being trolled by homophobes. What do you do?' (Stay calm, delete hate speech and do not feed the trolls!)

'You can choose one celesbian to put on the cover. Who do you pick?' (The hilarious national treasure that is Miriam Margolyes. Can you imagine how much fun she'd be to interview??)

'We are now leaving you alone in this room for ten minutes to write a column on how they're killing all the lesbian characters on TV.' (Synchronize watches. Lez go!)

I want this too much. I'm so nervous, my voice seems to be coming out funny, sort of strangulated and wobbly. I try to rescue the situation by making a joke about it. When they ask what my biggest weakness is I reply, 'Caring too much . . . as you can probably hear from my voice!' Thank god, they laugh. It breaks the ice and diffuses my anxiety.

I leave the office unsure of how I've done. I think I gave some good answers, but I can't say for certain. It's all a bit of a blur.

I don't hear anything for a week. Oh well, I tried. I got myself in the room. That has to count for something.

And then I get the call. I get the call while I am at my reception desk, serving my notice period. I rush into an empty meeting room and try to stay calm and composed.

I've only bloody got the job.

As soon as the call ends, I can't help it. I well up. I have cried so many times at this office, but never happy tears until this moment. I am soaringly happy. I feel like I've been handed a ticket to a life I have been chasing for so long. After a decade of struggling and applying and pitching in vain, of wondering if I'll never make it in a creative career because 'Who cares what some random dyke has to say?' at last I have found a place that values my voice, as both a writer and a lesbian.

So, I am finally feeling more optimistic about the future. I don't want to give the false (and frankly, dangerous) impression that it is work that rescues me from my demons. I quickly discover that the DIVA job, although exciting, creative and fulfilling, is also intense, gruelling and at times very stressful. But for me personally, this moment in time when I finally get the gig that means something to me, this act of reclaiming control of my own life, is powerful.

My queer career move reframes my sexuality, taking the very thing I have felt such shame about for so long and forcing me to appreciate the joy in it. It makes me feel like part of a wider community and grounds me with a sense of purpose.

It also marks the final shedding of my childlike instinct to desperately try to win praise from my parents. I am, after thirty years, letting go of that pernicious, people-pleasing impulse that has always lurked inside me. Accepting this job is, in a way, an act of defiance. In a world that tells me my sexuality is wrong, I am doubling down on my queerness. I am throwing myself into a career that I know could never make my parents proud. But that no longer matters quite so much, because do you know what? It makes me proud.

First day at *DIVA*: a to-do list

1. Obviously, workshop perfect outfit. Style inspo: queer spin on Carrie Bradshaw's working at *Vogue* era? Lesbian spin on Lois Lane?

2. Plan commute, allowing extra time for TFL disruptions and wardrobe malfunctions. Remember to take safety pins!

3. Set alarm. Music to wake up to – Dana International: 'Diva'.

4. Set back-up alarm in case first alarm fails. Back-up music to wake up to – Girls Aloud: 'Wake Me Up'.

5. Pack new rainbow pencil case with rainbow pen, rainbow rubber, rainbow notepad, highlighters in assorted rainbow colours . . . on second thoughts, maybe not.

6. Research lesbian news. Find out exactly what's going on for lesbians right now and think of intelligent opinions about it all. Can I come up with any homosexual hot takes??

7. Prep pitches for magazine features, online articles and social media posts. Go in armed with shedloads of ideas and enthusiasm.

8. Practise Shari's power pose thing to channel Wonder Woman/Goddess energy.

9. Prep packed lunch. Rainbow salad maybe? Is that a thing? Overkill? Reminder: be cool!

10. Note to self: you worked hard to get here. You got the job. You can do this.

CHAPTER 20

The dawn of a new DIVA

Appropriately enough, I start my job at *DIVA* just in time for Pride month. On my first day I arrive at the North London office half an hour early, so I sit on a bench on Hampstead Heath until it's time to head in. When I do, I'm all aflutter, eager to make a good impression and scared in case I put a foot wrong and blow my big chance. Nervously, I walk into the open-plan office *DIVA* currently shares with *Gay Times*. The *DIVA* team is sitting in the far corner, which is decorated with giant blown-up pictures of iconic *DIVA* covers.

My first day flies by. There are so many new colleagues to meet and there's so much information to take in. I am put to work writing a piece about the singer Ladyhawke, and tasked with coming up with pitches for a topical opinion piece to run in the print magazine. 'The print magazine!' I think excitedly. The same print magazine I found in WHSmith before I'd even come out.

Talk about being thrown in at the deep end: on my second day I'm assigned a press junket with the cast of *Orange Is the New Black*. I'm a big fan of the show, Netflix's flagship women's prison drama featuring a diverse cast of characters, many of them queer.

When I step out of Charing Cross tube station, I'm bricking it. I locate the venue, a luxurious five-star hotel, and head to the check-in room. A hotel suite adapted into a holding pen for journalists, it's full of calm, collected pros. I bet they've all quizzed a thousand celebs in their time. As for me? I feel like an imposter, like Hugh Grant in *Notting Hill*, getting flustered interviewing Julia Roberts and pretending to be from *Horse & Hound*.

I'm shown into a private hotel room to interview Selenis Leyva and Kate Mulgrew, AKA Gloria and Red. I'm almost shaking with nerves, clutching my notebook filled with the questions I've come up with after hours of research. The interviews all go well, thank goodness. As I exit the fanciest hotel I've ever stepped foot in and walk through the centre of London, I look up at the majestic buildings and the clear blue sky, and I think to myself, 'What is my life?'

The *DIVA* job is exhilarating, but there's a lot of hard graft and long hours too. It is not a nine to five. I'm working evenings and weekends to meet all my deadlines. The workload is high and the pressure is on. One of the bonuses of the relatively small team is that my duties are unusually varied for an entry level role. I get to do everything from admin tasks such as sourcing images for articles, responding to reader queries and scheduling social media posts, to more appealing assignments like reviewing queer films, working at photo shoots and writing longread features. I say yes to everything.

I work my arse off and, in time, rise through the ranks. I am promoted from editorial assistant to staff writer to deputy editor to managing editor. My role is always wildly varied. One day I might be in the office, participating in pitch meetings and crafting articles. Another day I might be at a big event. Like the time I'm working at the *DIVA* Music Festival.

❋

It's the closing night of the four-day event held in a holiday park in Dorset and the headline act, singer-songwriter KT Tunstall, is onstage wearing red leather trousers. The opening bars of coming-out anthem 'Suddenly I See' blast out and the already pumped audience instantly goes up ten notches. A consummate pro, KT struts around the stage, commanding the room, belting out her smash hit with aplomb.

At the end of the song, the crowd goes wild. In a final flourishing gesture, KT tosses her guitar plectrum up in the air and out to the cheering audience. Everyone scatters and scrambles, desperate to locate the keepsake. These superfans are on a serious mission. We're talking crawling-around-on-the-floor levels of dedication to the Tunstall treasure hunt.

I look down, wondering if it landed anywhere near me, and suddenly I see: KT Tunstall's plectrum is nestled in my cleavage. Alarmed at the possibility of a pile-on, I make a sharp exit. I will cherish this plectrum. Cheers KT.

✤

On another *DIVA* field trip, I spend a day with the London chapter of the legendary Dykes on Bikes, interviewing them for a feature in the magazine. I've been longing to ride with the real-life Dykes on Bikes ever since I discovered they were a thing at Sydney Mardi Gras all those years ago. That first time I saw them, they were electric. So powerful. So proud. So instantly iconic. I wanted to be as badass as them. Today, I am an honorary member of their esteemed tribe.

'Do I look butch, babes?'

I stride around our flat, wearing Naomi's leather jacket and my best Danny Zuko pout.

'Is that my jacket?'

'Yes. Does it make me look butch?'

Shimmying my shoulders like a lesbian Elvis, I swagger

around performatively. I exude bravado. She squints at me, confused, then laughs.

'Why are you walking funny?'

'It's my butch walk, babes! Is it working?'

She does not seem convinced. I look at her solemnly.

'Do you think I should lose the pink handbag?'

Forty minutes later, I'm ready to meet the gang. On balance, I decided to keep the handbag. Who says you can't be a dyke on a bike and also enjoy a dash of pastel? Entering the open-air bikers' café in Epping Forest, I see tattooed guys in black leather and hear engines revving.

I glance around nervously. Then I spot a group of women in leather jackets emblazoned with rainbow flag patches and badges saying everything from 'Trans rights are human rights' to 'Suck my clit'. Ah! My people! Far from being Hells Angels, they are the warmest, gentlest, loveliest ladies. Ranging in ages from thirties to sixties, most of them are barefaced with cropped hair, and have an irresistibly chivalrous old-school butch quality.

They have all given each other special biker nicknames. There's the Parisian Petit Chou, with short pink hair and a mischievous grin. A six-foot-tall plumber called Badger: it's a long story, involving 'a badger the size of a feckin' horse'. And then there's the preschool teacher who goes by Slick. 'My name begins with "S" for Su, and . . . I like to lick.'

The club secretary, Pogs, rocks up on her Harley Davidson. 'The granny of the group,' quips Petit Chou, a nod to Pogs being in her sixties. Pogs is quite possibly the coolest person I've ever met. 'Don't worry,' she reassures me, taking off her helmet like a rock star. 'We're all pussycats.'

They tell me about the origins of Dykes on Bikes, how it all began at San Francisco Pride in 1976. They talk about the power of lesbian visibility, the unrivalled camaraderie, the freedom they feel as a sisterhood. Slick invites me to try out her enormous bike for size. I clamber aboard, straddle and rev the engine. The whole motor vibrates intensely between my thighs. Ok, now I understand why they do this every weekend. Who needs a rampant rabbit when you have a machine this powerful?

After the safety briefing, we set off for our ride. I climb on the back of Badger's bike and cling to her for dear life. We ride through the forest in staggered formation. Then suddenly we're soaring down the open road, a band of sisters in unison. My nerves evaporate so all I'm feeling is exhilaration. My senses are magnified. The trees have never looked so green. The sky has never been so blue. I can feel the kiss of the breeze against my skin. Cruising with my homos, I bask in the moment. I am utterly alive.

❉

While working at *DIVA*, I see queer culture metamorphosize, expand and gather steam until it explodes. Suddenly in the late 2010s it feels like queer women and non-binary people are everywhere. I am here to document each moment, from pop star Janelle Monáe wearing pink vagina pants in their music video to Sally Wainwright's BBC period drama *Gentleman Jack*, about real life nineteenth-century diarist and 'first modern lesbian', Anne Lister.

That's why, on this late summer day, Naomi and I are on a sapphic pilgrimage. When the opportunity arose to review a *Gentleman Jack* minibreak for the magazine, naturally I snapped it up. The show, and Anne herself, make me feel proud to be a Yorkshire lezza.

So we have headed to Halifax to visit her historical home, Shibden Hall, AKA the mothership. We aren't the only ones. Thanks to *Gentleman Jack* and Suranne Jones' breathtaking performance in the starring role, Anne has won herself an army of loyal Lister Sisters. There are lady-loving ladies everywhere I look, poring over portraits of their patron saint and getting flustered over her bedroom. I wonder what she would make of all these women fangirling over her stately home. I bet she'd bloody love it.

This place is positively steeped in herstory. If these walls could talk . . . Well, they can talk actually. These walls have talked, because Anne's extensive journals were discovered hidden within them. Her diaries contained all her innermost thoughts, including details of her numerous romantic encounters with other women. Much of the content was so scandalous she wrote it in a secret code. (Fun fact: Anne had a niche hobby of saving tendrils of her lovers' pubes in lockets as sexual souvenirs.) It is in this house that she wrote words so potent they reach out through time and make us feel things in the present. Words like her immortal line: 'I love and only love the fairer sex.'

Once we've explored the house, we do our best Anne Lister power dyke marches around the grounds to find a suitable bench for our picnic lunch. We look out over Shibden Park. The view is spectacular: Anne's home in the foreground bordered by flowerbeds, then rolling green fields and endless sky above.

The heavens open. We do not move. We stay there, huddled together under one umbrella, munching our sarnies. As we are the only people bonkers enough to be dining in a downpour, we have it all to ourselves. Two Northern lesbians who grew up under Section 28, utterly unaware that all this queer history was right here on our doorstep. Our hands find each other. We breathe in our heritage, the nature and the epic gayness of it all. As we gaze out peacefully on the same rainy vista Anne must have looked at all those years ago, we make-believe that this is our home.

❊

The following February I am on a press trip to Sydney, working on a travel feature about the Sydney Gay and Lesbian Mardi Gras. I'm back in my sort of second home for the first time in nine years. It always seemed like an anomaly in my life story that I lived here. I'm not remotely surfy, not exactly back-packery. I grew to love Sydney though. I became attached to its sun-drenched streets and queer community and the way the ocean laps the city centre. It is bound up with so much of the formation of my identity. It's where I went to my first Pride. It's where I lived with my first love.

Being back here again feels significant, cinematic, a full-circle moment. Sitting at the Opera Bar in Circular Quay, I look out at that postcard picture come to life. The Harbour Bridge with retro funfair Luna Park peeking out underneath, the elegant explosion of domes that is the Opera House, and the vast expanse of water that is restless, never still. I'm not sure how I thought I'd feel being back. I thought I'd prob-ably feel a lot. Sitting here now, I start to feel absurd – staring at landmarks, waiting to emote. It must be a good sign that I'm not a sobbing heap. And this is with jetlag. Who knew I could be so emotionally controlled? Maybe I'm all cried out over everything that happened back then. Perhaps I'm finally at peace with the past.

I get up off the designated emoting chair and retrace my old footsteps. As I rove around the gaybourhood, I smile at the rainbow zebra crossing, at the drag queen dressed as Wonder Woman, at the off-licence sign that says 'Lick-Her Here'. Passing my favourite local gay bookshop, still thriving after all this time, I pop in to buy an anthology of lesbian erotica as a souvenir.

Before I know it, it's the day of the Pride parade, twelve years after the first one I ever experienced. And now I'm marching alongside a squad of drag queens with matching beehives on a magenta *Priscilla Queen of The Desert* float. We have attended dance rehearsals to perfect our routine. I bust out the choreography and add a few flourishes of my own for good measure.

Suddenly I find myself in the middle of Oxford Street, right near the Stonewall Hotel. I realize this is almost the exact same spot where I watched my first Pride freshly out of the closet. I stand still, just for a moment. I look around and drink it all in. This is the ballroom and battleground of my youth. It is in this moment that the emotion that wouldn't come before floods me. But it's not sadness I'm feeling. What I feel is gratitude, for this place, and these people, and how far I've come since being that wide-eyed twenty-two-year-old girl.

Back then, I was watching the parade from the sidelines; now I am in its flow.

A (true) entry from my diary, aged thirty-four

Granny, it's been five years and I still miss you every day. The more time that passes, the longer I have had to live in a world without you in it.

I miss visiting you. I miss getting dressed up for you in something elegant and stylish. I dressed for you, more than I dressed for anyone else. I miss telling you my news. I could tell you much more exciting stories now, about working at a glossy magazine, writing articles and travelling the world on press trips. I wish I could tell you my news and I wish I could hear yours too. I wish you could meet Naomi.

Sometimes I worry that the day you died, so did a part of me. My spark, my fire, my dazzle. I want to get back to that joie de vivre, but it feels hard because, in so many ways, you were my joie de vivre.

How do I move forward? How do I let you inspire me and enrich my life, even though you are at rest? I know the answer. I must honour you through my own life. I must channel your iridescence. I must do my best to shine like the sun, as you did. I must be glamorous and gutsy and always interested in life, as you were. I must keep talking to you. That's what you did after Grandad was gone.

Be more Granny. That's my goal.

CHAPTER 21

The power of community

I'm checking in my luggage for my flight home from Sydney, when I notice the alarming number of people around me wearing masks. Walking through the airport feels eerie. I've read bits and pieces in the news about a new virus, but I haven't begun to grasp its severity until now.

Just weeks later, it is clear that we are in the grip of a global crisis. Naomi and I watch Prime Minister Boris Johnson on TV as he announces the first Covid-19 lockdown. Both our phones immediately start pinging with back-and-forth messages from concerned family and friends. As the pandemic progresses, we monitor the rising death toll, feeling both deeply saddened and profoundly unsettled. People start using previously foreign phrases like 'social distancing', 'support bubble' and 'let's schedule a Zoom'.

As for our relationship, we are very fortunate in that we do pretty well when it's just the two of us. We both worry a lot about the world and our loved ones and the future, but we find comfort in being together.

One day when we're masked-up and out on our daily walk around the block, I realize that spending this much time together doesn't feel like a struggle. In every other romantic relationship I've had, I always needed time for myself away from my partner. I think that's a totally natural thing to feel and I wonder why I don't feel it with Naomi. Maybe it's because with her, I can be my whole self in every iteration from dancing queen to goofball to professional go-getter to quiet or sad or ruminative. I do not worry that she will judge or reject me. And if for some leftfield reason she ever did, I know I would not stand for that now.

At work, we're all feeling the pressure. We're currently working from home, but advertisers have been pulling out of the magazine due to the pandemic and I'm worried this might be what sends *DIVA* under. Then at the end of April 2020, I'm furloughed along with the rest of the permanent editorial staff, and printing the magazine is paused. I don't know if *DIVA* will survive all this. And if it doesn't, where will that leave me? Best add that to the long list of anxieties currently running through my head on a loop of doom.

I know I should be using all this time indoors to my advantage, to write and get fit and learn a new language. But instead, here I am in the middle of the day, obsessively refreshing *The Guardian* homepage for the latest horrendous headlines while panic-necking bucketloads of wine. The subsequent hangxiety does not help matters. I do my best not to dissolve into a quivering heap with varying degrees of success.

❋

It takes months, many months, but furlough finally ends. *DIVA* is still standing and I am back at work. Well, kind of. Everything looks different. The office is no more. I still go into town for meetings, interviews and events, but the day-to-day is remote. After paying London rent but not being able to enjoy London for so long, Naomi and I start contemplating giving up the big smoke and heading for the seaside.

Both well into our thirties and fully committed to this

relationship, we'd love to start saving up for a deposit. There's no way we can afford to do this in London. The cost of living is prohibitively high. This city has been my home for ten years, but maybe it's time to say goodbye and start working towards putting down permanent roots with the love of my life. Then one day, pretty much on a whim, we do.

Hastings meets our two non-negotiable requirements of being on the coast and a relatively cheap train fare away from the capital. So, in hope of a fresh start with fresh air, we bundle all our belongings in a van and set off towards the sea.

The day I find out I've been promoted to editor-in-chief, Naomi and I drive to the ocean. We look out on it from a clifftop country park and I feel so many feelings. Excited about the possibilities, nervous about what lies ahead, but passionate about bringing my vision to the magazine in a meaningful way. Then I laugh at myself. I'm forever gazing out on a body of open water emoting like a buffoon. But there it is. That's me.

✻

Every week is hectic when you work at *DIVA*, but no week is quite so hectic as Lesbian Visibility Week. Boy, is it exhausting being visible! There's no time to be tired though, because tonight is the thirtieth anniversary *DIVA* Awards. This independent magazine has been here, being ever so queer for three whole decades. I do my soundcheck on the stage in preparation for the speech I will give later on. I have done this several times before, but tonight it's that little bit more special.

It's not all glitz and glam though. Now I'm getting ready for the big night in a toilet cubicle. I pull on my metallic 1940s gown, a nod to the sapphic starlets of yesteryear like Tallulah Bankhead. Unlike Tallulah, who as we've already established famously loved to cartwheel into parties commando, I am firmly encased in a massive pair of pants. No fanny flashing here. I am nothing if not a professional.

Naomi is with me, the woman who carries my heart and my bags. We head to the main entrance to greet guests as they arrive. Everyone looks fantastic. Sandi Toksvig is rocking the hell out of her sequin blazer. Broadcaster Adele Roberts and her partner actress Kate Holderness are the perfect power couple in coordinating monochrome. And activist Eva Echo is an absolute showstopper in the most spectacular, cascading orange dress, embroidered with powerful messages from members of the trans community. The place is packed with trailblazers and icons. Even Dannii Minogue, host of hit new sapphic dating show *I Kissed a Girl*, is here to celebrate the moment.

We're called in for dinner and before I know it, it's almost time for my speech. As observed by my granny when I was a little girl, I can deliver the goods but only if I go into a corner first and get myself into the zone. Knowing me just as well as Granny did, without me having to ask Naomi tactfully excuses us from the chattering crowds and guides me into the next room where it's quiet so I can focus.

And now I'm up on stage addressing the audience. I read out some of the many heartfelt messages I've received from our readers about the role that *DIVA* has played in their lives.

'*DIVA* was my beacon through many a storm.'

'I'm a trans dyke and I love your mag.'

'I'm so grateful to *DIVA* for making me feel seen.'

'Long may *DIVA* transform lives!'

I think about the role that *DIVA* has played in my own life. From discovering it all those years ago when I was trapped in that shame-filled closet, to being right here now as its editor-in-chief, in this room full of love and pride and pure queer joy. I am not alone. None of us are. I look out at this beautiful crowd full of unique, beaming faces and I know that there is nothing wrong with any of us. We are together, we are a community, and we are magnificent.

❖

One of the great privileges of working at *DIVA* is the opportunity to have in-depth conversations with so many exceptional women. I don't want to bang on about celebrities, but I do want to talk about one very special interview that happens a few weeks after the awards.

Today I am interviewing literally my dream interviewee for the cover of *DIVA*. She's an actress, a memoirist and a renowned maker of mischief. She is, of course, the outrageous, the sensational, the one and only Miriam Margolyes. The Cadbury Caramel Bunny herself.

We sit together in the study of her South London home for an hour, just the two of us. We are surrounded by her many well-thumbed books, family photographs and all the artefacts she's collected throughout her extraordinary eighty-three years on this planet. Our wide-ranging discussion spans career, parents, politics and more. We talk about the joys of lesbian sex, her fifty-five-year relationship with her partner Heather, and that time she posed starkers for *Vogue*, save for a pearl necklace and a pair of strategically placed iced buns. She tells me, 'I'm gay and I'm really pleased I am. I wouldn't be straight for anything.'

When she's not making penetrating eye contact with me, she gazes around her office pensively. She surveys its many treasures, as if contemplating all that has happened in her life so far. Ever the show woman, sometimes she slips out of ruminating mode and bursts into a spontaneous one-on-one performance of her favourite Charles Dickens characters from her new Edinburgh Fringe show.

Miriam is inquisitive and wants to know about me, in my experience an unusual quality in an interviewee. This is how I find myself talking to the BAFTA-winning legend about my magic grandparents with their mind-reading act. Her own grandfather was a magician, so she absolutely loves this gem of family lore. 'How marvellous!' she declares. I tell her that the way she speaks about her mum, as a beloved cornerstone figure in her life who has helped shape the person she is to this day, that is how I feel about my granny.

It is a deeply moving experience, having a heart to heart with this remarkable, hilarious, wise and wonderful lesbian in her eighties. And just when I think it can't get any better, something truly incredible occurs.

Oh my, I honestly can't believe that just happened. I feel so lucky right now.

Reader, she farted.

Miriam is famous for her fondness of flatulence and she executes this one with impressive precision. Just before she lets rip, she leans forwards a little in her chair and says, calmly and factually, 'I'm going to fart now.' Then she lets one off, grins at me mischievously and purrs, 'Isn't it gorgeous?'

'Oh, Miriam!' I exclaim, utterly delighted. 'You have just made my day. There is no one in the world I would rather pass wind in my presence. Now I feel I've had the whole Miriam experience.'

'Well,' she chuckles. 'Now you've had the lot.'

Who would have thought a career highlight could involve an octogenarian celesbian cutting the cheese?

Confessions of a professional lesbian

Close your eyes and imagine a magazine editor. Are you picturing Anna Wintour from *Vogue*? Or maybe Meryl Streep in *The Devil Wears Prada*? Sorry to puncture the fantasy, but editing an independent queer publication is not remotely like that. There are moments of preposterous glamour, but mostly it's rolling up your sleeves and grafting as hard as you can with limited resources to try to create something meaningful for your community. Outrageously, you get sent literally no free designer clothes. On the bright side, publicists will merrily dole out complimentary sex toys till the cows come home.

Working at *DIVA* I may not have the front row seat at fashion week, but I do get a front row seat to all the good, exciting, joyful things that are happening for our community. Let me tell you, there are hundreds. Progress is possible. There are so many reasons to be optimistic and hopeful for a brighter, more inclusive future.

Working at *DIVA* I am also among the first to hear about the horrifying news, the hard-won rights being rescinded, the global atrocities. Let me tell you, there are thousands. While progress is possible, we cannot take it for granted. Yes, we have come a long way, and we should and must celebrate that. But there is so much work still to be done to ensure that the brighter, more inclusive future becomes the reality.

This job teaches me many things. One of the most powerful is the realization of just how big our community is. One of the most devastating is the realization of just how divided we can be within our own ranks. The transphobia, the racism, the ableism, the biphobia. This kind of prejudice where queer people turn on other queer people is so misguided, heartbreaking and dangerous. The perpetrators are projecting their anger in the wrong direction. Save all that rage for the real enemy. Channel it into dismantling the patriarchal structures that continue to oppress all of us, including you. If you know what it is to feel shamed and unsafe, as all women do, as all queer people do, why would you persecute others who have felt that pain too? Compassion, empathy and active allyship are vital. We are so much more mighty when we stand united.

I am lucky enough to interview hundreds of remarkable creatives. I have discovered that the number one reason incredible queer people make groundbreaking books, shows, films and music is to create the representation they desperately needed when they were younger but did not see. In doing so, they heal something deep within themselves, while also healing others like them.

I have never met a queer woman or non-binary person who felt sufficiently represented by the media. Without exception, we all feel underserved. This experience can be even more acute for those with intersecting marginalized identities, for queer people of colour, trans folks, disabled sapphics, intersex lesbians, asexual people or those who are neurodivergent and LGBTQIA. Sharing our stories is vital. It lets other people and ourselves know that we are not alone. We always need more stories. We need an ever-expanding vault of unique, nuanced, intersectional stories, because representation is magic. It changes lives. It even saves lives. If you don't see yourself represented, create that visibility yourself.

There is no right way to be queer. The whole point of being queer is to be your truest self, whatever that looks like. By the way, there is no right way to be a woman either.

It's all well and good meeting celebrities, but nothing gives me quite such a rush as hearing from a reader who has been impacted by the work we do. I have been that reader. I know how precious that feeling is. Having come full circle and seeing it from the other side? That's the real thrill.

After growing up in a world that taught me to feel ashamed, and a decade navigating offices dripping in casual misogyny and homophobia, being in a workplace surrounded by other queer people, in an environment where queerness is emphatically embraced, is profoundly healing. If only all workplaces could be so inclusive.

It is a rare privilege to actually feel fulfilled by your work. But it *is* still work. In fact, being passionate about what you do can make you more prone to slip into patterns of overworking, stress and burnout. You are no use to anyone if you don't look after yourself. Get fresh air, move your body, rest and reset. Remember, you are not your job. You are so much more than that.

Although it is healing in so many ways, work is not the thing that saves me. Maybe it is love that saves me. Love and women. Not necessarily romantic or lesbian love. The relationships I have had with remarkable women, whether a partner, friend or family member, have brought the most strength, meaning and beauty to my life. Those women, who love and embrace me just the way I am, who bring me back to myself as I do them, they are the ones who got me through.

CHAPTER 22

What this girl wants

When we moved away from the hustle and bustle of city living to make a new life together on the coast it was, to be honest, an impulsive, ill-thought-out decision. Prior to relocating there, we had only visited Hastings once. We knew there was a gay bar and we'd vaguely heard about an event called 'Queer On The Pier'. We hoped that meant it was queer-friendly. Mostly, I really liked that it had so many antique shops and you could get an off-peak return train ticket to London for under thirty quid. But we hadn't done much research beyond that. We figured we could try it for a year, save up, get more fresh air and then reevaluate.

Three years later, we are still here. After scrimping and saving for a deposit, we are at long last able to buy a place to call our own. Our modest flat is a twenty-minute walk from the sea and has its own garden. It's not perfect, but it's ours. When we sign the final paperwork and collect the keys, I feel emotional. At last, I am putting down permanent roots with my person. We are a tiny family of two. It feels like we are taking a step to look after each other as we grow older.

I have never felt so at home in my own home. Not in the house I grew up in, not even in my beloved bedsit, liberating though it was for that period in my life when I so desperately needed to carve out my own space. The only other time I've felt this kind of comforting domestic warmth was as a little girl staying over at my grandparents' place.

Being with Naomi has never been the hard part. Being with Naomi is the thing that has made all the hard parts that bit more bearable. During our time together, we have nursed each other through illnesses, bereavements, family issues, work stresses, redundancies and more. Every one of those challenges would have been so much harder to face without the support of each other. When external factors have been gruelling, Naomi has helped keep me grounded.

So have my dearest friends, who always bring me back to my essence when I feel like I'm starting to flail. Just last week I was out for dinner with Lela. After knowing each other for more than twenty years, we're still the best of pals. There we were in a fabulously maximalist restaurant, counselling each other through our troubles, getting the irrepressible giggles, and ooh-ing and ah-ing all over the extravagant décor.

Once we'd finished our meal, we popped to the ladies together. Immediately, we were awestruck by the stunning interior design. Pink roses decorating the ceiling, elaborate mosaic tiles on the walls, and – ding-ding-jackpot – exceptionally flattering lighting. We looked at each other and exchanged a giddy grin. And so, an impromptu photo shoot began, just as it has on so many occasions over the past two decades. It quickly descended from posing, pouting and smiling prettily to pulling the most ridiculous faces we could conjure to make each other laugh with abandon. At heart, we are still the same glamorous goofballs we were at sixteen.

I laugh all the time with Naomi too. If we do ever argue, it's usually over something ridiculous and it tends to coincide with a classic case of PMT squared. One of the biggest fights we ever had was back when we lived in the tiny London bedsit. We were both due on, which never bodes well.

Looking around, feeling irritable and overly stimulated by my daring interior décor choices, Naomi asked, 'Does everything *have to* be hot pink?'

Naturally, I was mortally wounded. My hormone-addled brain took deep personal offence. In my head, I catastrophized the comment to a slightly mad degree.

'How dare you use pink against me? Don't you come for my core.'

Oh dear. Roxy's triggered!

I was so distraught and our flat was so tiny, I had to lock myself in the shower room until we both calmed down. Needless to say, this squabble didn't last very long and in our new seaside home we've compromised on the colour scheme. While there is still an excessive amount of pink, it's now in shades of rose and cherry blossom which, if I'm honest, is a lot more relaxing.

In the kitchen-living room, there is a blush velvet sofa bed that took us yonks to pay off, but was worth every penny because now whenever Lela, Shari or Jess come to stay they have somewhere cosy to sleep. On the antique drinks trolley in the corner sit two framed photos. One of my granny, looking like a wartime pin-up in a one-piece bathing suit, her curls pinned back from her face, posing on an unexploded bomb. She and Grandad found it on the beach and decided it was the perfect prop for a photoshoot. They don't make them like they used to.

Next to it is another framed photo of me, Naomi and her family at her brother's wedding. That was a golden day filled with love and laughter. I always remember us being at the evening disco with Naomi's mum and sister. When 'This Is Me' from *The Greatest Showman* came on, I turned to see her mum Angela, shoes kicked off, dancing her heart out. I knew she was my kind of woman. Naomi looked at us both going for it on the dancefloor, carefree and loving life. She quipped, 'I'm basically going out with my mum.'

Naomi and I have been together for almost a decade now. How do you make a long-term relationship work? It's like my granny said. We are great friends. We laugh together. We support each other. I know how rare that is. I know how lucky I am. We still really fancy each other too, which helps. Naomi never fails to grab my bum when I'm walking up the stairs. I take this as a sign that our relationship is still going strong. And twenty-five years later, two and a half decades since I was that shame-filled schoolgirl, it is still just as thrilling to kiss a beautiful woman. Even more so, because this one is my person who I love not just behind closed doors, but out in the open too.

So, what does this girl want? Well, I want the world to be a kinder, safer place for me, my partner, for women and for every member of my glorious, diverse community. I want to never again feel like I must make myself less so that others will love me more. I want all that toxic shame to go away for good. And I want you to know that whoever you are, however you identify, whatever your body looks like or craves, you are worthy. You are wonderful. And most of all, know this: you are loved.

Epilogue

It's a spectacular August day at the seaside. The sun is shining. The seagulls are keeping a respectful distance. The tide is coming in and Naomi is butching it up on the barbecue.

Today would have been my granny's birthday. When I was a child, we always celebrated it with a trip to Runswick Bay on the Yorkshire coast. We paddled, we picnicked, we had fish and chips in Whitby for tea. In the years since she passed, it has become a private tradition for Naomi and me to spend this day at the beach, in memory of my sunshine girl.

This has become significantly more convenient since we moved to live by the sea.

'A seal!' I suddenly shout. 'I see a seal!'

I pass the binoculars to Naomi in excitement and point in the direction of my discovery.

'I don't think that's a seal, babes,' she says kindly.

I look again, twizzling the lens adjuster, concentrating hard.

'False alarm,' I sigh. 'It's a . . . bit of floating wood . . . I think.'

I watch with fondness as Naomi returns to her culinary task. The sausages are burning and we never do spot that seal, but it is one of those perfectly imperfect days.

When I was a closeted teenager growing up in Leeds, wrestling internalized homophobia, puberty and patriarchal bullshit, I could never have imagined I would end up here. Editing the same magazine I used to read in secret. Sharing a flat with the woman I love. Mistaking driftwood for ocean wildlife.

In some ways, I'm the same person I was at thirteen. I'm still women's number one fan. I'm still a sucker for silliness. I still go weak at the knees when my girl looks at me a certain way. Yet when I was thirteen I was, in so many ways, a stranger to myself. I was brave enough to do covert sapphic snogging at every opportunity, but too terrified and indoctrinated to dare to seriously think about what this might mean.

I know myself better now. I know that it does not serve me to fear what I want and who I am. I know that I need to run towards my passions, desires and dreams, not away from them. I know that you can only fight the fibre of your being for so long, before it starts to destroy you. I know that it is the system that is broken, not me. After all those years swimming in shame and self-loathing I've finally accepted – no, embraced – both my sexuality and myself.

I wonder, if I could clamber into a rickety time machine and travel back to offer teenage me some sage, hard-won, queer elder wisdom, what would I say? The answer arrives instantly. I would urge her to, for god's sake, quit people-pleasing and stop prioritizing others' comfort over her own happiness. No doubt younger me would nod gravely. She'd give the impression that she was really taking everything I was saying to heart, that she thought I was ever so wise and profound with terrific dress sense, because she could tell that this reaction would please me most. And then she'd continue on her people-pleasing, closeted, clumsy way. Some lessons have to be lived to be learnt.

But while I had her attention, I might also casually bring up her colossal crush on Jet from *Gladiators*. And, as long as it didn't disrupt the space-time continuum too drastically, I'd accidentally-on-purpose let it slip that her beloved high-kicking, hair-flipping, leotard-sporting 1990s TV personality is now married to a woman. What can I say? I like to spread queer joy wherever I can.

Back on the beach, we nibble the edible bits of our sausage sarnies and raise our paper cups of wine high. I make a toast to my favourite girl with my other favourite girl. We look out at the vast expanse of ocean and the rugged cliffs in the distance and the gorgeous, ripening sunset. The whole sky is the most beautiful shade of pink. In this moment right here, I am serene, I am myself and I am home.

Acknowledgements

Firstly, thank you to my brilliant agent Laura Macdougall. Your advice is invaluable and I love that I get to work with such a powerhouse in publishing. Thanks, as well, to the wonderful Eleanor Horn and Olivia Davies at United Agents for all your assistance.

To the phenomenal Jodie Lancet-Grant, thank you for your belief in me and this book, and for encouraging me to dig deeper. You truly are the editor of dreams. I'd also like to thank the amazing team at Bluebird, Pan Macmillan, including Sian Gardiner, Megan Tanzer, Maya Conway, Laura Marlow, Mia Lioni, Siobhan Hooper, Katy Denny, Cara Waudby-Tolley, Annie Rose and Kathryn Palos.

Thank you to everyone at *DIVA*, past and present. Thank you Chance Czyzselska for giving me my first proper job in journalism. Thank you to the awesome Team *DIVA* including Linda Riley, Nancy Kelley, Fiona Marshall, Fernando Safont, Nic Crosara, Ella Gauci, Char Bailey, Ellen Tout, Yasmin Vince, Ali Morgan, Kellie Lombard and Rachel Shelley. And a special thank you to *DIVA*'s incredible readers.

To my gorgeous friends, thank you for the love and laughter. Darling Lela, since we met at the age of sixteen you have enriched my life beyond measure. Magnificent Shari, thank you for making me both giggle uncontrollably and dare to dream bigger. Jess, you glorious, creative goddess, you bring me so much joy.

To my family, I love you. To Angela, Mark, Nicola, Jonathan, Sarah, Ivy and Beau, thank you for all your kindness and for welcoming me with open arms.

To Naomi, you are quite possibly the world's most supportive girlfriend. Thank you for making me laugh so hard and for loving me so beautifully. You are the wind beneath my wings and the hand on my bottom.

And finally to you, lovely reader, thank you for taking the time to read my story. I really do appreciate it.